BRING YOUR OWN TECHNOLOGY

The BYOT guide for schools and families

MAL LEE AND MARTIN LEVINS

ACER PRESS

First published 2012
by ACER Press, an imprint of
Australian Council *for* Educational Research Ltd
19 Prospect Hill Road, Camberwell
Victoria, 3124, Australia

www.acerpress.com.au
sales@acer.edu.au

Edited by Ronél Redman
Cover, text design and typesetting by ACER Project Publishing
Cover images © ipixs, James Thew, Mike Flippo, mkabakov and Shutterstock 2012
Printed in Australia by BPA Print Group

National Library of Australia Cataloguing-in-Publication data:

Author: Lee, Malcolm, 1944-

Title: Bring your own technology : the BYOT guide for schools and
                 families / Mal Lee ; Martin Levins.

ISBN: 9781742861005 (pbk.)

Notes: Includes bibliographical references and index.

Subjects: Educational technology--Australia.
                 Computer-assisted instruction--Australia.
                 Information technology--Study and teaching--Australia.

Other Authors/Contributors: Levins, Martin.

Dewey Number: 371.3340994

FOREWORD

Jill Hobson

The recent eruption of interest in Bring Your Own Technology/Device, or BYOT, within the educational community has led to a number of news articles, blog posts, tweets and status updates. Yet, BYOT still seems a 'bleeding edge' concept for some. The hubbub seems to be very heavily focused on BYOT as a technology hardware initiative, with less consideration for the instructional impact that BYOT *should* be facilitating.

BYOT can bring about transformational instructional activities. When a teacher transitions from saying, 'Everybody is going to build a fill-in-the-software-name-here project' and starts saying, 'I need you to demonstrate that you have learned the concept and how you can do that using your device', then transformation starts to happen. A natural differentiation takes place when students can choose how they represent their learning!

In my own district, the technology leadership team began planning for and considering the infrastructure, policy and instructional practices that would be needed in a BYOT environment as long as ten years ago. And one thing I know for sure is that out there on the bleeding edge there are no maps, no case studies, nowhere to turn for guidance—it's make-it-up-as-you-go.

Thus I'm so excited to have one place to go for a comprehensive look at BYOT from an international perspective! This guide provides a thorough rationale, plus case studies, and examines the underlying pedagogical strategies that will make such innovations successful once implemented. The authors set this book apart from the rest of the BYOT conversation by examining this new concept from all directions and, most especially, from the instructional and pedagogical point of view. For all those who are contemplating BYOT or are already on the path, *BYOT: A guide to introducing a 'Bring Your Own Technology' model* provides a wealth of information to drive your program to great success.

Jill Hobson is the Director of Instructional Technology for the Forsyth County School District in Georgia, USA. This school district is showing the way in the astute introduction of BYOT.

CONTENTS

ACKNOWLEDGEMENTS

The authors would particularly like to acknowledge the great support provided by Chris Hubbard in the USA and Terry Freedman in the UK.

We would also like to thank Jill Hobson, the Director of Instructional Technology in Forsyth County, Georgia, USA, for writing the Foreword and for the wonderful support she and her Forsyth County team provided in the researching and the writing of the book.

When venturing into uncharted territory it takes a particular type of leader who is prepared to overcome the inevitable travails of the unknown. The leadership was evident in all the case study schools, both by the principal and the key senior staff. It is, however, important to make particular mention of the following people, who helped to provide an insight into the workings of the case study schools: Corrie Barclay, Tim Clark, Tim Ennion, Adrian Francis, Trevor Galbraith, Duncan Gillespie, Kim Head, David Hounsell, Suzanne Korngold, Sue Lowe, Bailey Mitchell, Frank Pitt, Debbie Smith, Bradley Tyrell, Leanne Windsor. Their support was supplemented by the expertise of Ken Price, Bernard Ryall and Lorrae Ward.

To Greg McKay, whose graphics provided the book with a particular lift and character, we say thank you.

As ever, thanks to the wonderful editorial team at ACER Press with whom, once again, it was a pleasure to work.

Mal Lee and Martin Levins

INTRODUCTION

THE TREND

The trend line strongly suggests that in time every school in the developed world will use some type of 'Bring Your Own Technology' (BYOT) model of school technology resourcing, where the students use their own personal technology in the classroom. For some schools that will be years from now, but it is highly likely that eventually even those schools seemingly entrenched in their paper-based teaching will go digital, normalise the technology's everyday use, begin to genuinely collaborate with students' homes and to start using a form of BYOT as they recognise the wisdom of integrating the approach into their operations.

It appears it is a case of when it will happen, not if.

THE NAYSAYERS

We recognise that there are naysayers and indeed strong critics (Speirs, 2010; Stager, 2012) decrying the mere idea of BYOT. But you will appreciate the paucity of the call made by these folk when you understand the:

- strength of the global forces impelling schooling inevitably on this course;
- natural adoption that flows when schools normalise the use of the digital;
- logic of letting the market shape the choice of personal digital technology in schools; and
- plethora of potential educational, social, economic, political, technical and organisational benefits of BYOT.

1

As with any other fundamental organisational change, that is not to say there aren't significant issues to be addressed and pitfalls to be avoided. But as the developed world has consistently shown, astute minds will address those issues. Naysayers expressed the same concerns about the movement of banking and finance online, and there have been and will continue to be significant issues in that arena that have had to be and inevitably will need to be addressed. But capable people have been able to resolve most of the problems and to fundamentally change those industries.

The same acumen is already evident in the pathfinding schools that have integrated BYOT into their operations. We hope you will do the same and take note of the relevant research, the experience of the case study schools and the advice and issues addressed in the following pages. All too often when many hear of the BYOT concept for the first time, they jump in and become instant experts without sufficient knowledge about it. They'll then explain why the move is detrimental. Others who have given the concept a little thought view it simply as a technical development that can be safely left to the ICT staff. Perhaps not surprisingly at this stage in history, many of the early BYOT moves are naive and simplistic, preoccupied with the relatively mundane and showing little appreciation of its BYOT's within the wider educational scene.

POTENTIAL IMPLICATIONS

BYOT is shaping up as a profound educational development with immense potential that will in time assist in fundamentally changing the nature of schooling and teaching, the school technology support model, school resourcing and schools' educational relationships with their students and their homes.

Bailey Mitchell, the long-time Chief Technology and Information Officer for Forsyth County in the USA, observed that the introduction of BYOT into the County was 'one of the most exciting things I've ever seen' (Mitchell, 2012). The challenge from the outset is to see BYOT as an integral part of the evolution of schooling that can markedly assist your school in providing a quality education for a networked world. It is not just about the technology or improving student performance; it is about the totality and how the development fits seamlessly in schools operating within a networked paradigm.

For too long, too many in key positions have approached the improvement in schooling by viewing schools as insular and segmented organisations where, by improving one segment, the whole school performance will be enhanced. In the digital and networked world, schools are ever-more tightly integrated organisations where virtually all the boundaries of old, even the walls separating the school from its community, have been removed and all the parts are interrelated.

In contemplating the introduction of BYOT it is vital from the outset that you view it as from a helicopter, looking at the total scene and considering how its introduction will impact on all the workings—human and technical—of your school and its community. Gone are the days of approaching the development with a silo-like mentality.

Talk with the system and school leaders within Forsyth County and you will soon recognise you are talking to a group who are addressing the introduction of BYOT from a holistic perspective, who appreciate how the development fits with the County's educational vision, who understand in contemplating BYOT that you need to simultaneously address the educational, administrative, technical, financial and political elements and how they will best integrate all the developments into the school's and the County's overall program.

BYOT requires sophisticated thinking and astute leaders, willing to lead.

KEY ELEMENTS

In contemplating adopting a BYOT model, three major components must be addressed. The first, which is the focus of most of the current writing, is why your school should make the move. The second, which has received no mention but which ought to be considered in conjunction with the first, is the readiness of the school to successfully accommodate the development. The third, which has also received scant attention, is what you need to do from the outset in your implementation to enable the school to transition from its current personal technology resourcing model to one where 100 per cent of your students use BYOT as a normal part of all school operations as soon as is feasible.

Think carefully about the kind of base you need in order to prepare for BYOT to quickly disappear from the school's vernacular and for it to become as normal, invisible and all-pervasive as the use of the pen and paper.

Part of a total educational package

The first and overarching imperative is recognising that the adoption of BYOT is an educational issue to be woven into the everyday teaching and learning of the school and all support operations.

Home–school collaboration

Closely allied is appreciating that the normalised use of BYOT is going to require a far higher degree of genuine collaboration between the school and the home than is to be found in the vast majority of schools today. BYOT is already appearing to be part of the suite of dividends flowing seemingly naturally to those pathfinding schools operating within the networked mode that have normalised the use of the digital, are collaborating closely with their homes and have adopted a more collaborative mode of teaching and learning. BYOT involves the home and the school genuinely working together. Those schools are pooling the resources of the school, the students' homes and their community and making smart use of the digital across the total school community every day and throughout the year—24/7/365.

Mal Lee and Lorrae Ward are working on complementary research on collaborative teaching (Lee & Ward, forthcoming). It explores an approach to teaching which pathfinding schools operating in the networked mode across the developed world are moving towards to better educate their students for today's world. It is based on a close and genuine collaboration between the home and the school. It recognises that many people teach young people from birth onwards—the parents, often the grandparents, and in time the professional educators, community members and, importantly, the young people themselves.

Collaborative teaching means the professional teacher teaches the key educational building blocks in partnership with the young person's other non-professional teachers, recognising that each will have different areas of prime responsibility and will use different teaching styles, and that in most areas of learning the most effective teaching and learning occurs when all the teachers of young people work together.

Fundamental to the 24/7/365 collaborative teaching is that the students, the parents and particularly the professional teachers have normalised the use of the digital in their teaching and operations and have ready access—anywhere, any time—to the digital (Lee & Ward, forthcoming). It recognises that the young people of the developed world use their suite of digital technologies to teach and learn, and in doing so since the mid-1990s have developed a universal mode of teaching and learning suitable for the networked world.

It also understands that the teaching and learning model of the place called school is still predominantly paper-based, is insular and teacher-dominated and struggles, despite the rhetoric, to accommodate the digital and the networked, even to acknowledge the nature and impact of the teaching and learning happening outside the classroom and shift to a mode appropriate for the twenty-first century (Lee & Finger, 2010).

Importantly, these schools also recognise that their students have to succeed in the student assessment challenges set by their nation, be it basic skills testing, A levels, SAT or securing appropriate tertiary entrance scores, but believe that this too can be provided in a holistic education. They appreciate that there are many in government, academia and school leadership positions today who still believe an appropriate education for the twenty-first century involves simply a focus upon and success in a small group of academic subjects, that the success of a nation's education of all its young people can be measured by its international PISA scores and that there is nothing to be gained from the teachers collaborating with anyone other than their colleagues within the school walls. Those believers basically dismiss any conscious teaching of the thinking, digital, social or emotional skills and attitudes—those twenty-first century skills—deemed fundamental to success for all the young people at school, in life and at work so strongly advocated by the major employers and educationalists (like the Partnership for 21st Century Skills, Bellanca & Brandt, 2010).

Sadly, in reality that is generally what has transpired in many schools until recent years.

While John Dewey powerfully articulated the necessity of democracies providing an appropriate holistic education near on a century ago (Dewey, 1916) and presciently warned of the need to factor a consideration of the formal and informal into the curriculum in what he saw as a time of rapid technological change, we have today in most schools a growing home–school digital divide (Becta, 2009b), with the formal schooling being regarded as increasingly irrelevant.

The Illinois think tank on digital schooling, which included leading business management thinkers like Charles Handy and Gary Hamel, noted the following five years ago.

Kids lead high-tech lives outside school and decidedly low-tech lives inside school. This new 'digital divide' is making the activities inside school appear to have less real-world relevance to kids. A blend of intellectual discipline with real-world context can make learning more relevant, and online technology can bridge the gap between the two.

Illinois Institute of Design, 2007, p. 24

Authentic home–school collaboration is still a rarity (Mackenzie, 2009; Estyn, 2009). An occasional talk with some of the parents is not real collaboration. Despite calls for home–school collaboration by public policymakers for years, most schools operate alone behind their walls, having only a tokenistic liaison with students' homes. Significantly, that is changing virtually overnight in those schools that have normalised the use of the digital across the school and have adopted the more collaborative mode of teaching described above.

One of the unintended dividends of home–school collaboration and the pooling of their resources and expertise appears to be the natural shift to BYOT (Lee & Ward, forthcoming). Why that is so research has yet to explain, but in the case study schools operating within the networked mode in the USA, the UK, New Zealand and Australia examined by Lee and Ward, all had or were about to adopt some form of BYOT. Significantly, none of those schools had planned on using a BYOT model. It simply occurred when they moved into the networked phase of schooling. For example, Forsyth County in Georgia, USA, one the lighthouse users of BYOT globally, did not plan for BYOT; the development flowed naturally—and initially unwittingly—from the use of the digital and the collaboration with the homes (Hobson, 2012).

For BYOT to work to its best advantage it should be considered as part of the broader home–school collaboration, where the parents and the students as owners of technology need to be convinced that the school and all its teachers want to collaborate in making best use of that technology and are prepared to listen to and act upon the home's desires. There is an old but still apt adage that he who pays the piper selects the tune. A number of schools and education authorities would do well to remember this before adopting a 'one-way collaboration' approach that tells the parents and students what technology they have to provide and instructs them how their technology will be used in the school and under what conditions. In its 2010 study of home–school collaboration,

Futurelab (Grant, 2010) not surprisingly identified the long-term damage incurred by such an approach.

Authentic collaboration implemented wisely can provide that rarity—a win/win for all the parties—the parents, students, school, education authority, politicians and taxpayers. One-way collaboration might (and we stress *might*) provide short-term wins to the school and authority, but will most assuredly provide significant losses to the clients and increasingly the taxpayers. The 'one-way collaboration' approach accurately indicates a school's or education authority's lack of readiness to realise the immense potential of BYOT. It shows a continued operation within an insular, paper-based mindset. That thinking must change to make astute use of BYOT.

Admittedly, the whole notion of a school or authority needing to be ready to use BYOT hasn't yet appeared in any of the literature or plethora of blogs on BYOT. At this stage most of the thinking and writing in relation to BYOT and schools is limited; it has no research base and comes primarily from those with an interest in the technology rather than from the whole-school development or public-policy perspective.

Readiness

As you read this book you will come to appreciate there is a significant suite of key readiness factors (see Chapter 4) that warrants your careful consideration before making any BYOT moves. Two of the most important at this stage in the thinking appear to be the readiness of the school's teaching staff to genuinely collaborate with its homes, and the professional teacher's willingness to use a style of teaching that will convince the students it is worth taking their personal digital technology along to that teacher's class.

As mentioned, the first factor is closely tied to having all, or at least a critical mass, of the teachers in the school having normalised the use of the digital in their teaching (Lee & Finger, 2010). The second is apparent in all the case studies but again rates no mention in the current literature. In reality it should come as no surprise that the students won't bother taking their technology to class when it is going to sit idle; it is what we would all do. The teachers therefore have not only to have normalised the use of the digital and be of a mind to collaborate, but must also be using a teaching approach—a pedagogy—that makes use of sophisticated digital technology. The latter is not a black-and-white issue, nor is it a reason for holding back on introducing a BYOT approach, but it is an issue that will have to be addressed if your school is ever to achieve sustained, 100 per cent BYOT usage.

Another important variable that also appears to have been forgotten in the literature and is lost on some schools and authorities, is the imperative of each student to use the personal technology they want and which they believe will best fit their own style of learning, over and above the other functions they require of the technology. As we discuss later, there is much to be said for schools offering advice on which technology students might aptly use. However, as we also note, the track record of many schools in this area is not glorious and there is much to be said for students and families proving the school wrong or learning from their poor choice. From the education perspective, there is also much to be said for students with their different learning styles using the technology that suits them best.

Let's be clear. Long gone are the days when the technology performed but a single function. We are talking about a suite of ever-evolving, ever-more sophisticated, increasingly convergent, multipurpose digital technologies whose scope is being broadened daily with new apps that will be used in teaching and in life. We are also increasingly likely to be talking about the individual's desired mix of mobile digital technologies, not just one device.

BYOT should not be confused with the 1:1 computer thrust, for while it is intended that every student would have their own technology to use anywhere at any time, they will be using their own suite of technology and not simply a single computer. Such thinking is dated.

Students are already using their technology 24/7/365, teaching themselves (probably with the help of their peers), learning all manner of things and using all the devices they have whenever they desire. Disturbingly, the classroom is probably the one place where they are not using the technology.

While it might come as a surprise to some educators, the school use of the digital by young people represents but a minor part in the total overall usage. They are already using the technology to personalise their teaching and learning. With BYOT, they will be looking for the school to support that personalisation and the facility to use their preferred personal mode of learning.

CONCLUSION

Your challenge is how do you convince the school community to ready itself to take best advantage of the BYOT development to understand the value of being proactive to appreciate the plethora of opportunities potentially offered by the development and to recognise what the school and its community have to do to make the most from the adoption of a model of BYOT.

....

BROULEE PUBLIC SCHOOL

Situation

- Broulee Public is a state school of around 300 Kindergarten to Year 6 students that serves a coastal village in regional New South Wales (NSW), Australia. The school is a four-hour drive south of Sydney, well away from any large city support.
- Broulee is part of the NSW DEC, one of the larger and more centralised education authorities in the developed world, where the school has limited control over its resources and limited say in its staffing.
- Socioeconomically, the student group falls just below the Australian norm.

Fuller details on the school and its program can be found at:
http://www.broulee-p.schools.nsw.edu.au/Home.html.
Contacts: Sue Lowe, Principal or David Hounsell, Assistant Principal (A/P)

BYOT developments

Broulee is one of the first schools in NSW to adopt a model of BYOT, the development flowing naturally from the school's normalised use of the digital by all staff and the school's close collaboration with its community.

Broulee has provided all staff with their own laptops since 2000. Since 2010, it has had IWBs and pods of iMacs or MacBooks in all teaching rooms as well as additional IWBs and more than 30 other iMacs in its iCentre and suites of iBooks and iPads for use by all classes. For the last decade, the school has provided wi-fi access across the campus.

The school has used its normalised use of the digital as a base to develop a more collaborative mode of teaching with its homes, a comprehensive digital communications suite and its model of BYOT. While senior education authority officers have shown significant interest in the school, no additional educational or technical support has been provided in the move to BYOT.

Broulee first began its BYOT moves in late 2011 after discussions with the Year 4, Year 5 and Year 6 students regarding their preferred model, and with the parents and the staff.

Under the leadership of the principal and the AP, the school opted to start with Year 4–6 students. The school chose to start with a written policy, closely akin to what the students suggested, which required that the parents affirm their readiness to take the technology to school (http://www.broulee-p.schools.nsw.edu.au/Information_for_Parents_files/BYOT%20Policy%2012.pdf).

The student uptake was particularly pronounced from the start of the 2012 school year, with many of the classes fast approaching total student uptake.

Interestingly, perhaps as a long-standing 'Apple school', the students have opted in the main to bring their own Apple iPod touches and iPads. The contrast with Coal Mountain Elementary (p. 20), which was a 'Windows school', is pronounced; there the students have chosen a far more diverse mix of Android, Apple and Amazon technology.

CHAPTER 1

BYOT AND ITS SETTING

The concept of BYOT is still in its formative stage. While there is increasingly more talk of the students bringing their own technology into the classroom, our research could find virtually nothing written on fleshing out the concept or defining what is entailed. We found little effort had thus been made to place the development within its wider societal or school development context.

If one is to approach the introduction of BYOT astutely, it is important to clarify what BYOT is—and what it is not. It is also vital to address the development in context, both as part of the wider change within society and industry and within the school's own setting. The following is designed to provide that understanding.

BYOT—A DEFINITION

The authors offer the following definition to fill the current void.

> *Bring your own technology (BYOT) is an educational development and a supplementary school technology resourcing model, where the home and the school collaborate in arranging for students' 24/7/365 use of their own digital technology/ies to be extended into the classroom, and in so doing to assist their teaching and learning and the organisation of their schooling and, where relevant, the complementary education outside the classroom.*

Fundamental to BYOT are:

- Personal choice of the technology by the student or family; while schools might (and probably should) provide advice, the final choice should rest with the home
- The enhanced facility for the personalisation of teaching and learning inside and outside the school walls
- Recognition that the in-school use of the students' digital technology is an extension, a flow-on development from their existing use of that technology to assist their self-teaching and learning
- The home and students having their ownership of the technology and the information stored thereon respected.

As indicated, the research is already highlighting the importance of authentic home–school collaboration to the school achieving normalised usage of the students' technology. However, one can opt for a model of BYOT (as indicated in Chapter 5) where there is minimal collaboration and where the school or education authority largely unilaterally informs the parents what they are obliged to do with their personal technology, although the signs are already suggesting that the likelihood of schools realising many of the outcomes identified in Chapter 3 by adopting such an approach appears to be small.

There are a number of so-called BYOT initiatives that pay scant or no regard to personal choice, do not recognise that students will want to work with the personal technology they are already using every day, do not respect the parents' or students' ownership of the technology, basically don't trust the students and are not seeking to personalise the teaching and learning. In these instances, under the banner of BYOT, they are using an imposed compulsory buying scheme, not much different from requiring parents to buy students' textbooks.

Note that in doing your own research into BYOT, you will come across the terms 'BYO', 'BYOC', 'BYOD' and 'personal digital devices'. They are to all intents and purposes the same thing. The reason we prefer 'BYOT' is that the term 'technology' neatly covers both the hardware and the software and the fact that the students could, and are increasingly likely, to use multiple digital technologies. The simple 'BYO' (bring your own) isn't specific enough (we are not talking about beer!); 'BYOC' refers specifically to the use of computers and is thus limited, as is 'BYOD' with the reference to devices but not the vital software. That said, we will not be manning the barricades to defend the term 'BYOT', but will most assuredly be supporting the key elements of the concept.

A brief but important note to add is that the focus of this book is the personal digital technology that can be used across the curriculum, and not the specialist technologies required in particular areas of learning like digital photography, programming, industrial design and high-end media production. (Those needs are addressed in Chapter 8.) We will be talking about the general tools of the 'trade' and not those of the specialist.

THE SETTING

In looking at the desired BYOT model, bear in mind the kind of networked world young people will be operating within—digitally based, rapidly evolving, ever flatter, more collaborative and integrated, where learning is no longer restricted to a physical place and where the divisions and walls of old are daily being dismantled.

> It's when a technology becomes normal, then ubiquitous, and finally so pervasive as to be invisible, that the really profound changes happen, and for young people today, our new social tools have passed normal and are heading to ubiquitous, and invisible is coming.

> Shirky, 2008, p. 105

Indeed, in 2012, young people's use of the digital has virtually become invisible.

We are talking about the networked world explored in depth by Lee and Finger in their work on developing and leading a networked school community, where the schools that have normalised the use of the digital are beginning to pool their resources with those of their students' homes to provide a significantly richer, more relevant, effective and holistic education (Lee & Finger, 2010). (A shorter discussion of the type of networked school community where BYOT will be employed can be found at http://www.malleehome.com.)

We are also talking about an ever-flatter world of the type popularised in the writings of Tom Friedman. His seminal work, *The world is flat* (2006), examined in some detail the impact of networking and the technology upon the world since the early years of the twenty-first century, the removal of the traditional barriers to competition and the opening of the way for all the world's nations—in particular, the emerging mega-powers of China and India—to use the bandwidth and cyber world to compete on a largely level footing with the powers of old. It is a world where the signs are strongly suggesting that 'stand-alone', insular schools working behind their school walls will struggle to continue shutting out the real, networked world.

Schools globally are finally evolving and after centuries of relative constancy and continuity are becoming digital. While teaching in most is still predominantly paper-based, virtually every school in the developed world is making ever-greater use of the digital and, like the pathfinders, will in time normalise the use of the digital.

Once organisations go digital, be they banks, travel agencies, hospitals or schools, they quickly leave the traditional constancy and move into a world of ongoing evolution and often rapid change shaped increasingly by the ever-emerging technology, they begin to dismantle their traditional internal and external walls and start to network (Lipnack & Stamps, 1994). That is what has happened with the pathfinding schools globally (Lee & Finger, 2010). Daily, more are moving to the networked phase of their evolution where they have normalised the whole-school use of the digital and are using that technology to collaborate ever-more closely with their homes and community.

A significant but still very new concept for educational administrators is emerging: that this changing organisation needs the freedom and time to grow and evolve. Traditionally, educational administrators were schooled to maintain tight control over all facets of a school's development. That was appropriate in an era of constancy and continuity where the desired nature of the school had been well researched. But when schools move into the digital mode and are working with constant and often rapid uncertain change, it becomes increasingly apparent that the school leaders need to cede some of that control and be prepared to let the organisation grow and evolve.

Both the collaborative teaching discussed earlier and BYOT, as indicated, appear to be a natural evolution from schools normalising the use of the digital. Significantly, the leadership in many of the case studies have noted the development and are providing their authority or school the time, freedom and flexibility for BYOT to grow and take form.

This evolution of schooling is happening at the same time as the digital and educational capacities of the students' homes are burgeoning, the use of the digital is becoming all-pervasive in life and work, and the expectation is that the mobile technology of young people will be used astutely 24/7/365, including in the classroom (Chapter 3).

In terms of BYOT in schools globally we are still at an early stage, but the speed of uptake is so rapid across the developed world we would use the metaphor of the tsunami on the horizon to describe the current situation. As the uptake of the various personal mobile technologies escalates and becomes ever-more sophisticated, and the number of educational apps available for use with those technologies burgeon, likely so too will the magnitude and power of the 'BYOT tsunami'.

What is important to appreciate is that the move to use one's own technology everywhere is happening in every facet of life, work and education. The BYO moves in business are already pronounced and when one looks at virtually any university campus today, one will find the students using all manner of personal technology.

In 2009, Lee and Ryall (2010) examined the concept of 'bring your own' (BYO) in schooling and flagged the considerable benefits of its adoption. Importantly, they explored in some depth the potentially considerable economic benefits of the move for schools, education authorities, local and national governments and taxpayers.

At the outset and in the definition we have stressed that BYOT is a significant educational development which, when introduced astutely, will impact markedly upon the nature of schooling and teaching and on the relations between the home and the school. It does also have the potential to markedly change not merely the nature of school technology funding, but indeed the recurrent resourcing of schools. It is important to understand that facility.

However, to fully appreciate that potential change, particularly if you are not involved with schools, you need to appreciate a couple of key facets about the present mode of school resourcing across the developed world.

The current model of school resourcing basically emerged in most developed nations in the latter 1800s at a time when few families had any teaching capability in their homes. Most in society had to send their children to school to be educated; in turn, the 'state' (that is, some level of government) provided all the funding required to conduct those schools. Across the English-speaking world, the call was for schooling to be free—a call that continues today, although we all know that increasingly that is not so and that for some time parents have had to put their hands in their pockets.

The other important facet of school resourcing you need to appreciate is that the vast proportion of recurrent funding provided by government to the schools goes on staff salaries. While the figures vary, in general terms near to 85–90 per cent of the annual income is spent on staff. Significantly, that percentage has, as Perelman (1992) noted, been rising since the 1950s with the quest to secure ever-smaller classes. It would be a brave government, local or national, that sought to reverse that trend and use larger classes and fewer teachers. The likely reality will continue to be that schools will have to pay for all their other needs from the remaining 10–15 per cent of the recurrent allocation, be it toilet rolls or the latest technology.

As the general funding pool remains static or is shrinking, in real terms the digital and educational capability of the students' homes is burgeoning. In examining the digital technology available to an average Year 6 class of 30 students in Australia at home and at school, Lee and Ryall (2010) found that availability in the home was on a conservative estimate 15 times greater than in the classroom. Not a factor of 2 or 3, but 15-plus. Lee and Ryall suggested that the time had come for government to appreciate that the situation today differs greatly from that in the 1800s and that the school-resourcing model needs to reflect that change.

Globally, governments are struggling to provide schools with the funds to remain current with the personal technology they provide, at a time when the vast majority of homes already have that technology and more. Since the GFC, even the wealthiest of nations are struggling to find the money and, as the proportion of the aged population grows, will continue to do so.

As we elaborate in the next chapter, there are compelling economic reasons—among the many others—for governments, education authorities and indeed taxpayers to support BYOT. The important thing is to appreciate that in so doing, schools will be inexorably moving to a fundamentally different model of both school technology and school resourcing. BYOT makes a major (but we'd suggest logical and pragmatic) educational shift consistent with an increasingly networked and collaborative world, to a public/private/community funding model that proclaims a new, tighter nexus between the home and the school in the holistic teaching of young people, and which in turn ought to move the 'free' mandate of old to the historical archives.

It is appreciated there will be those vehemently opposed philosophically to the change. However, one does have to understand the ever-changing context and that the reality is the pathfinding schools have already set that change in motion. The tsunami on the horizon will make the change inevitable. The key is to shape the change as one desires.

THE NOW

At the time of writing, the literature available to guide you on the use of BYOT is limited in the main to blogs and some education authority websites. It is by its nature short and light, based strongly on opinion, with scant supporting research. Significantly, the writing focuses on the impact of BYOT on the teachers. We could find nothing that addressed the introduction of BYOT from a client's perspective or explored how the parents or students might feel about or benefit from the move. It was almost as if it was of no concern to them, even though they were expected to fund the development.

The tertiary sector literature is significantly more research-based and, although focused on a different teaching and learning environment, does provide some valuable insights. The writings of John Traxler (Traxler, 2010a; 2010b) are well worth a read.

This book is designed to help redress the shortage of in-depth analysis and advice for schools and authorities across the developed world. It is deliberately pitched at the classroom teacher and parents and although we have striven to build on a research base and to be scholarly, we have no desire for this to be the defining academic treatise. Rather, the intent is to provide, where we can, sound research-based advice to guide your way.

Early in 2012 we are seeing, in general terms, two main approaches among the early users of BYOT.

1   Those schools and education authorities working within the networked operational mode that have gone digital and are beginning to or have reached the networked phase on the school evolution continuum, are ready attitudinally and competence-wise to operate as networked school communities, and are naturally moving to pool the school and home resources. (Lee & Finger, 2010)

2   Those schools and education authorities that are instructing the parents and students as to what will be allowed in the school and what restrictions the students will need to work within. Some are also virtually prescribing which technology the students must use. Significantly, there is scant or no collaboration with the parents or the students.

In brief, we have two general approaches: one naturally evolving based on genuine collaboration and the other where those in control inform the clients what will be allowed. We will let the following chapters help you decide how effective each will be.

EQUITY AND COGNITIVE READINESS

There are two key issues we see as so important in relation to BYOT that we believe they need to be addressed at the outset: equity and cognitive readiness.

Equity

We are firmly of the belief that the education of every child is vital and that in seeking to shape the desired future, schools need to do whatever they can to:

- personalise the education of each child, and
- ensure that no one is disadvantaged technologically.

The bottom line is that the research strongly confirms the seemingly obvious: that students without home internet access are educationally, socially and economically disadvantaged and as such don't contribute as much as they should to the productivity of the nation (Becta, 2008; Chowdry, Crawford & Goodman, 2009). We realise there can never be a perfectly level playing field. There are simply too many factors impacting on success at school that are evident from conception onwards and are largely outside the control of the school. But the school, or the school working in collaboration with its community, government and/or business, should do its utmost to ensure each of its students has home internet access and use of an appropriate digital technology.

The market has gone a long way to reaching a price point where that is possible in every developed society. We're not suggesting the Aakash tablet is an iPad, but when India can embark on providing its millions of students with a web-enabled tablet for $US35 (and retail it for $US65), there should be few school communities in the developed world unable to assist those who genuinely cannot afford the technology.

The UK had for a time opted to use its national home access (Tolley, 2010) initiative to help redress the home shortcoming and in the USA, companies like Comcast are doing their bit to help. But regardless, upfront in your BYOT planning we would urge you to make sure that all your students who cannot find the funds are looked after.

We revisit this issue and look at possible solutions in the implementation chapters, but if your research (and not just a gut reaction) reveals that the number requiring support is too great to be resourced by the school or its community, we suggest you hold off until the school can find that support. Our strong suspicion, however, is that virtually all schools in the UK, the USA and Australasia have the wherewithal and are best placed operationally to look after those their communities unable to afford the requisite technology.

Cognitive readiness

In all the media hype about technology use by young people, there is a notable failure to heed the overwhelming body of research that affirms the young child's mind lacks the ability to think critically until around the age of ten. Until then, their use of the internet should be supervised by an adult.

> Always sit beside your child while s/he is on the computer and avoid thinking about the internet as a babysitter in the way that many parents do with television. Your direct and continuous supervision is necessary for teaching, to observe the behaviour of the child and protect your loved one. Before age 10 children lack the critical thinking skills needed to spend time alone on the internet.
>
> Strom & Strom, 2010, p. 69

The research is wholly in keeping with the studies undertaken by Piaget and many other developmental psychology researchers over the last 50 years. The bottom line is to strongly suggest primary schools should not consider a BYOT package that allows web access for children below the age of ten that does not include adult supervision. If you choose to do so, the risk you take is considerable.

CONCLUSION

In contemplating your school's or education authority's shift to a form of BYOT and considering the homework that is required, hopefully by now you will have begun to appreciate the imperative of recognising the likely profound educational and resourcing impact of the change, why it is a move not to be taken lightly and without due consideration of its potential, and what is required to realise that potential.

COAL MOUNTAIN ELEMENTARY SCHOOL

Situation

- Coal Mountain Elementary School is a public school of approximately 880 Kindergarten to Year 6 students, in Forsyth County, Georgia, USA.
- Coal Mountain is part of the Forsyth County School District and as such has considerable say over its staffing and its allocation of resources. That said, the school works closely with the County office and has long benefited from the leadership and support provided by the County, particularly in the use of instructional technology in the teaching and learning.
- Significantly, like the other Forsyth County case studies, the school has on staff both an instructional technology support teacher plus a media specialist.
- Socioeconomically, the student group falls pretty well on the USA norm.

Fuller details on the school and its program can be found at:
http://www.forsyth.k12.ga.us/Page/4183.
Contact: Debbie Smith, Principal

BYOT developments

Coal Mountain's move to a model of BYOT flowed naturally from the school's normalised use of the digital by all staff but, in contrast to most of the other case studies, was aided by the leadership and support provided by the local education authority's instructional technology unit.

The school has provided all its teachers with their own laptops for some time. Moreover, the school has had interactive whiteboards in all rooms since the mid-2000s, and all classes have ready access to an array of mainly Windows-based technology.

Importantly, like the other Forsyth County schools, Coal Mountain has had ready access to the internet, use of ANGEL, the County's learning platform, and in recent years wi-fi access across the campus.

Coal Mountain decided to make the first move to BYOT late in 2011 with two classes. At the beginning of 2012, it decided to involve 16 other classes and to let the development grow largely of its own volition.

The quality of the school's leadership, Debbie's grasp of the myriad variables that had to be simultaneously addressed and the school's willingness to collaborate with the central office were clearly evident in the interview.

While initially there were some parent concerns, the principal has been able to alleviate them.

Interestingly, in contrast to the Broulee Public case study (p. 9), the students' choice of personal technology is highly diverse, there being a mix of Android, Windows mobile, Amazon Fire and Apple technology.

CHAPTER **2**

CHARTING THE NEW TERRITORY

One of the obstacles in preparing to make use of the students' technology is the absence of any charts to show the way. No-one has travelled the full route and can talk about what is entailed in securing total student uptake, normalising the technologies' usage or realising all the opportunities on offer.

While some schools have begun the journey and some are well along the trail, in writing this book we were obliged to draw upon our own research and experience in the use of instructional technology in schools (Lee & Winzenried, 2009; Betcher & Lee, 2009), the research undertaken on the evolution of schooling (Lee & Gaffney, 2008; Lee & Finger, 2010), the experiences of the pathfinding schools and education authorities, and our own vision of the kind of route to take and the preparations to be made.

The decision to write this book emerged out of the work that Mal Lee did with Professor Glenn Finger on the evolution of schooling (Lee & Finger, 2010) and the recognition in 2011 that the theory enunciated by Mal Lee and Bernard Ryall (Lee & Ryall, 2010) on the economic wisdom of schools, education authorities and governments adopting a model of BYOT had already begun to become reality across the developed world. What hit home, aside from the pace and spread of the development, was that in many situations the adoption of BYOT appeared to be a natural extension of schools having normalised the use of the digital. What also resonated were the international forces at play impelling all schools towards the model and, approached astutely, the immense potential of the development.

CHARTING THE TERRITORY

The natural inclination when heading into new territory is to check what has already been written on the area. It soon became apparent that few of the writers had ever been into the new territory, let alone spoken to those who had. One was thus obliged to turn to the lessons that could be drawn from other areas, most notably the school use of digital technology and the impact of the digital on the evolution of schooling and teaching, both inside and outside the school walls.

In 2009, Mal Lee published with Dr Arthur Winzenried a study of the use of instructional technology in schools over the past century and identified what was required to achieve whole-staff 'digital take-off' and the normalised use of the digital. Initially, together with Professor Michael Gaffney (2008) and then with Professor Glenn Finger (2010), Mal Lee also explored the impact of the technology on the pathfinding schools across the developed world, and noted their movement from their traditional paper-based operational mode to one that was digital in nature and in turn based on a networked operational paradigm.

In brief, he explored the preconditions for BYOT and the kind of opportunities that opened up when a total school community normalised the use of the digital and the school and the homes pooled their resources and worked collaboratively for the students' benefit. That said, it was also vital to enhance that thinking with feedback from those making the early moves.

Much of that examination could be done online, scrutinising the websites of those schools and education authorities that have purportedly moved to introduce BYOT. A simple 'BYOT and schools' Google search provides a ready insight into the approaches that have been taken. Windsor's (2011) and Fisher's (2012) Scoop.it sites make it easy to view the current online writing.

What is particularly enlightening in the result of that kind of search is the wording of the BYOT usage policies that have been adopted by the various schools and education authorities. They succinctly communicate the school's or authority's approach to BYOT, the mindset it is working within, the nature of the collaboration with the parents and the trust it places in its students. While initially it might seem merely a point of semantics, note that many of the 'top-down' moves employ 'acceptable use' policies. The more trusting have tended to opt for 'responsible use' policies. The even more trusting don't even see the need to have a written policy.

But while insightful, there is only so much an online search can offer. It was vital to talk to those who were at least part of the way along the BYOT path and those in different situations.

THE CASE STUDIES

We sought out and obtained a cross-section of case study schools from the UK, the USA and Australasia. (As mentioned earlier, versions of this book have been prepared for the Australasian, USA and UK markets; thus our reason to draw case studies from all those areas.) All the chosen schools were given a common suite of questions and were then interviewed. Several related areas of concern soon emerged.

There was no common vernacular to guide the analysis of BYOT. In brief, there were schools claiming to be using a 'Bring Your Own Technology' approach where the school told the parents what technology they had to buy and have their children bring to school. To our mind, that approach did not embody the essence of BYOT. As there was no definition, we took the step of writing one (see Chapter 1, p. 11). It also became apparent, as indicated, that the schools and authorities were approaching BYOT from two fundamentally different directions. Both approaches provided important insights. There were also those schools that appeared to be travelling forward at pace and those that, for a number of reasons, were struggling to gain school-wide acceptance of the mode.

The more we delved, the more we saw the need to secure a better understanding of the seemingly natural flow-on effect being experienced by those schools that had gone digital. Collaborative teaching was found to be a natural flow-on from the school normalising the digital and working within a networked operational paradigm.

Was BYOT another flow-on?

Tellingly, all those schools and authorities that had begun the move to a more collaborative mode of teaching had also either adopted a model of BYOT or were about to do so. We thus added a number of those schools and authorities to the list of BYOT case studies.

Note that in the list of the case studies (Table 2.1) we have named all schools but one. After discussing the situation in the so-called 'School A' and noting the poor calls of judgement by the leadership, we thought it politic not to name the school or its location but simply to describe its situation.

Table 2.1 *Case study schools*

NAME	STATE/COUNTY	COUNTRY
Broulee Public School	New South Wales	Australia
Coal Mountain Elementary	Georgia	USA
Forsyth Central High	Georgia	USA
Kolbe Catholic College	Western Australia	Australia
Manor Lakes P–12 College	Victoria	Australia
Noadswood School	Hampshire	UK
South Forsyth High	Georgia	USA
St Mary Star of the Sea College	New South Wales	Australia
The Illawarra Grammar School	New South Wales	Australia
School A		Australia

THE FINDINGS

In working with the case study schools, the desire was simply to hear their stories and to learn of their experiences along the BYOT route so that we could identify any common experiences that others who are planning on travelling the route could benefit from. The aim was to learn from them and to pass on the lessons—positive and negative—to be borne in mind in your preparations.

As researchers, we were conscious of the newness of the development and its still nebulous nature, as well as the reality that sometimes the early adopter experience is not always applicable to that of the later adopters. That said, there are several general observations that can be made at this point.

The first, is the immense diversity of the case study schools; they come from the public, Catholic and independent school sectors and include primary/elementary/prep and secondary schools, small and large, urban and regional. However, the type, location or nature of the schooling would not appear to be a significant factor in a school opting to employ an appropriate model of BYOT. The fundamentals appear to hold in all situations. For sure, lack of bandwidth can be an influencing factor but that can still occur anywhere, even in the middle of a city and with any type of school. The students' technology was being used in every area of the curriculum. Forsyth Central, for example, found one of the more astute users of the technology was the physical education staff.

Importantly, no school had had to outlay any money on building alterations, particularly of the type needed with earlier digital instructional technology. Significantly, two of the case study schools were from a low socioeconomic (SES) area. The Manor Lakes case study (p. 68) is particularly pertinent in that it is a large K–12 public school in a new growth area with a sizeable lower SES group. While most (not surprisingly for early adopters) were in average to above-average SES communities, the case studies gave weight to the earlier-mentioned belief that in the selected nations virtually all schools can move when ready to a model of BYOT—bearing in mind the points made earlier about equity. None of the schools have completed the full 'BYOT journey', but several are moving at pace towards the 100 per cent student uptake.

Significantly, the case studies have identified a suite of key factors and opportunities not mentioned in the current writings that need to be borne in mind when charting your journey. As you will find in the later chapters where those factors and opportunities are examined in depth, some of the early movers have addressed them well, while others will need considerable remedial work before being able to move forward.

CONCLUSION

As we wrote this book, other case studies kept coming forward, offering to work with us in helping to chart the new territory. We are conscious (as are the case studies) that we are but early on in the journey and that, as we continue to talk, the way forward will become ever clearer. However, we feel confident that the insight already provided will help make your journey that much easier.

FORSYTH CENTRAL HIGH SCHOOL

Situation

- Forsyth Central High School is a public high school of approximately 2000 Year 7–12 students, in Forsyth County, Georgia, USA.

- As part of the Forsyth County School District, Forsyth Central has considerable say over its staffing and its allocation of resources. That said, the school, like the others in the school district, works closely with the County office and has long benefited from the leadership and support provided by the County, particularly in the use of instructional technology in the teaching and learning.
- Significantly, like the other Forsyth County case studies, the school has on staff both an instructional technology support teacher plus a media specialist.
- Socioeconomically, the student group sits above the USA norm.

Fuller details on the school and its program can be found at:
http://www.forsyth.k12.ga.us/Domain/1901.
Contact: Kim Head, Assistant Principal

BYOT developments

Like the other Forsyth case studies, Forsyth Central High School's move to a model of BYOT flowed naturally from the school's normalised use of the digital by all staff, but, in contrast to most of the other case studies, was aided by the leadership and support provided by the local education authority's instructional technology unit.

The school has provided all its teachers with their own laptops for some time. Moreover, all the teaching rooms are equipped with Promethean interactive whiteboards and in all there is ready access to an array of mainly Windows-based technology. Like the other Forsyth County schools, Forsyth Central has had ready access to the internet, use of ANGEL, the County's learning platform, and in recent years wi-fi access across the campus.

The school began moving towards a BYOT model in 2010 and since then has largely let the development grow. Not surprisingly, the model of BYOT that has evolved at the school is distinct and differs slightly from that adopted in the County's other high schools.

What came through in all the school's work in the area was the quality of the school's leadership, its appreciation of the plethora of human and technical variables to be addressed and its willingness to cede some control in order to let BYOT grow. From the outset the school saw the benefit of removing the angst associated with policing the ban on student technology, the impact of placing greater trust in the students and the improved student–staff relations that flowed from that trust.

Early on, the staff recognised the importance of adopting a more personalised style of teaching, prompted in part by the recognition that they could no longer rely on a common operating platform. At the time of writing, BYOT had become a natural part of the scene of the school, albeit with not all students as yet bringing their own technology.

CHAPTER **3**

RATIONALE

NOT IF BUT WHEN

Eventually all schools in the developed world will be using some type of BYOT due to the:

- confluence of powerful global megatrends
- natural flow-on effect from operating within a digital and networked operational paradigm
- ready facility of the market to accommodate rapid and uncertain technological change
- plethora of opportunities and potential dividends that will become available by adopting the model
- inevitable desire by schools to fall in line with their counterparts.

How and when you choose to address the developments in your situation is up to you, but one of the newer variables likely to impact on your operations is the growing digital empowerment of your community—your clientele—and their expectation that the school will collaborate with them and make astute use of young people's personal technology.

As you look ahead, the challenge is to appreciate why you ought to move, to recognise the abundance of opportunities to further enhance the school's effectiveness and efficiency, and to determine how you will explain the potential to others. In appreciating that potential, you should also better understand the kind of platform you will need for the eventual realisation of the full suite of outcomes.

At first glance, the rationale and thoughts on the potential benefits of successfully integrating a BYOT approach provided below might appear extensive. However, ours are preliminary ideas which will continue to be added to as schools globally push the boundaries, expectations rise, the technology becomes increasingly sophisticated, the research is undertaken, the collaboration between the home and school grows and everyone in the networked world becomes more accustomed to thinking in the networked mode. Our hope is that upon reading our ideas below, you too will think of other possibilities.

The history of the use of technology in schools over the last century is characterised (Lee & Winzenried, 2009) by the schools' and authorities' immediate focus on the actual technology and the facility of that new technology to enhance student learning within the place called school, and significantly the traditional kind of learning that pre-dated the advent of the new technology. The initial focus has always been on the technology—on the tool, per se—and seldom on the far more pertinent issue of how well teachers used that tool.

The same is apparent in the present writings on BYOT, even though it is talking about technology that is already being used 24/7/365 by young people everywhere but the classroom, and a mix of any type of mobile personal technology. The focus cannot be on the tool, because it is used in diverse ways, with different software, ever-evolving and in multiple forms. The implications of this new scenario for the style of teaching that should best be used (as the case study schools are finding) are pronounced.

In examining the potential opportunities offered by and the benefits of BYOT, it bears reiterating that one is analysing an ever-evolving suite of increasingly integrated multipurpose digital technologies, where many of the potential purposes have yet to be revealed. We are thus not merely contemplating the use of just a teaching aide but also the likes of an organiser, a communicator, a chronicler, a camera, a digital recorder, a multimedia editor and, when one adds the apps, any number of other facilities. Seek to take advantage of any or all of those facilities.

Moreover, try to envisage the kind of use with a networked mindset, asking how one can best take advantage of the students' ubiquitous use of the technology to enhance their holistic teaching and learning every day, all year round. It is a skill that takes time to develop. Within the insular paper-based mindset, teachers and administrators ask what they can do with the resources that they have been provided by their authority and largely dismiss any proposal that cannot be paid for from that source; within a networked mindset, those teachers and school leaders automatically ask what resources they have within their community that they can call upon to resource the proposal.

THE MEGATRENDS

Globally there are at least six key megatrends coming together that eventually will impact on every school, and pressure schools to make extensive use of the students' personal digital technology.

1   A global shift to an ever-more networked, collaborative, flatter and convergent world (as expressed in Friedman's *The World is Flat*), which is impacting upon every facet of life, industry and the service sector.

2   An upsurge in the use of cloud-based computing serving to dismantle the old divisions and flatten and integrate operations (NMC, 2011).

3   The movement of schooling globally from its traditional paper-based teaching and operations to one that is digitally based and increasingly networked (Lee & Gaffney, 2008; Lee & Finger, 2010). Schools, like all other organisations, are finally going digital.

4   The burgeoning digital resources and educative capacity of young people's homes and their normalised 24/7/365 use of the digital to assist their own teaching and learning (Lee & Levins, 2010).

5   A growing digital empowerment of young people and, more significantly, their parents and the growing willingness and expectation of both to use that power (Project Tomorrow, 2010; 2011; 2012).

6   The struggle of governments worldwide—financially, logistically and politically—to adequately fund the ever-evolving personal technology in schools. Where in the 1800s most homes lacked personal teaching tools and governments had to provide those resources, today the homes not only have the personal teaching tools while the governments are struggling to find them, but the trend is escalating in favour of the home.

You will undoubtedly be aware of most of these trends and thus we won't elaborate on all. But we do need to underscore several points that are particularly pertinent to the adoption of a model of BYOT.

You will be particularly aware of the extent to which young people have from a very early age normalised the use of the digital and how

31

theirs is a distinct outlook where they think networked (Green & Hannon, 2007; Tapscott, 2009). However, what might come as a surprise to some, particularly those not in schools, is how little recognition is given by most schools and education authorities to the extent, level and effectiveness of the teaching and learning that students experience outside the school walls. Since the mid-1990s and the advent of the World Wide Web, the young people of the world (the 'Net Generation'), with no help from educators, have developed a universal mode of teaching and learning (Tapscott, 1998; 2009) that suited their needs in the new networked world, while schools continued their reliance upon the traditional paper-based mode of teaching and largely rejected the digital developments outside the school walls. You will struggle to find an education authority or certification body that accords any recognition to the considerable self-teaching, peer teaching and learning young people the world over acquire in their all-pervasive use of the digital. Many educators dismiss this use of the digital as mere play, completely forgetting the research that affirms young people have long acquired their digital competencies outside the classroom (Meredyth et al., 1998).

Formal schooling constitutes less than 20 per cent of students' teaching and learning time each year (Lee & Finger, 2010). The use of the digital in that formal schooling is significantly less—well under half that figure. The remaining 80 per cent of the teaching and learning is left by default to the parents and students, with scant if any support or advice from the school (Lee & Finger, 2010).

Where young people outside the school have largely unfettered use of and operational responsibility for a sizeable suite of up-to-date digital technologies, in most schools (Maher & Lee, 2010) the use of the digital is still strongly limited by the number of teachers who have yet to normalise the use of the digital in their teaching, the limitations imposed on what type of technology is allowed, bans on student technology and the often strict controls on internet access. Ironically, while students are trusted with the use and care of all types of digital technology for at least 80 per cent of the time outside the school, in the classroom—the supposed place of learning—distrust is common, with often every minute aspect of student digital use being overseen by a teacher.

In relation to the parents and their digital capability and educational expertise, it is important to note that, historically, developed nations have never had such an educated cohort of parents or one that has largely normalised the use of the digital in their lives. Ever-more of the cohort are 'Net Generation' parents born after the mid-1980s (Tapscott, 1998) who expect that the digital will be used as a normal part of teaching.

The 2010 Project Tomorrow of some 42 000 USA parents noted that:

- approximately two-thirds of the parents planned to buy their children a personal digital device in the coming year and expected their school's teachers would collaborate with the home in the children's use of that technology in the classroom;
- they wanted to be the ones to purchase the desired technology, not the school; and
- while they wanted to collaborate with the teachers, if the school chose not to, they would use their own expertise to support their children's use of the digital.

Like all other developed nations, the USA now has a digital-empowered student and parent cohort with ever-rising expectations of schooling, increasingly willing to use their power (Project Tomorrow, 2011; 2012). Interestingly, the same survey noted that around two-thirds of principals said 'no way' to accepting their clients' wishes—that is, to the idea of using the student technology in class.

Most schools' ability to ensure all students have current personal digital technology is being made increasingly difficult by the growing pace of technological change; limited and often shrinking budgets; the reality discussed in Chapter 1 that 85–90 per cent of the recurrent funding is committed to staffing and onerous budgeting, buying and accountability procedures. Most employ some type of 'ICT expert' group to make those buying decisions, some of which get it right, but most appear to give little thought to the students' existing technology, the fact that the students will strongly tend to use their own, more powerful and current technology outside the school or that the school investment in technology might be significantly underused.

IMPACT OF OPERATING WITHIN THE NETWORKED MODE

As indicated, it is becoming increasingly evident that when schools operate within the networked mode—that is, have normalised the use of the digital in their teaching, have a student and parent community that has also normalised the use of the digital, have begun to dismantle the old school walls and collaborate with their homes and community in the

24/7/365 teaching of their students—the schools seem to move naturally to facilitating the use of the students' technology in class. It becomes apparent that it is the natural and sensible thing to do, rather than banning its use.

We appreciate that these are early days and greater research is needed, but daily as more schools begin operating within the networked mode they are likely to see the wisdom in collaborating with and supporting the students and their homes.

USE OF THE MARKET

From the early 1980s onwards, from the time of the Commodore 64, the Atari and the Apple II, parents' choice of personal digital technology has been shaped by the market. As the capability of the old is surpassed by the new, so the parents upgrade their gear (often at the behest of their children), ensuring in general terms that the technology their children are using remains current. By the mid-1990s, the market research was revealing that the vast majority of parents believed having internet access at home would enhance their children's educational development, making it increasingly important to have the current technology in the home (Lee & Winzenried, 2009). The same belief and reliance on the ever-evolving market still shape their buying today (ACMA, 2007).

In brief, the market determines when the Commodore 64s, the IBM clones, the CD towers, the brick-like mobile phones and the like will be moved aside for the new. That market-based arrangement historically has worked remarkably well in ensuring that young people have current technology in their homes—and increasingly in their hands.

In contrast, the personal technology acquired for use in schools, particularly within education authorities, has been selected not by the market but rather by the 'ICT experts' trying to identify what the market is likely to do. On reflection, there has been a cadre of astute operators, particularly within individual schools, whose choice of technology has been wisely influenced by the market; however, in researching the school technology decision making since the late 1970s (Lee & Winzenried, 2009), one has to conclude that in general terms most have done the job poorly and incurred immense waste of funds.

The 'ICT expert' model is increasingly displaying its inability to read and respond quickly to a rapidly evolving personal technology scene where 'game-changing' developments can now appear several times a year. When those experts enter an entire education authority into a four- or even two-year fixed contract, the students will be asked to make do with dated technology well below that which they already have. In contrast, the home, which doesn't have to wait for budget allocations, committee meetings, stringent buying and accountability procedures, can buy the latest technology whenever they wish (Lee & Ryall, 2010). Vitally, the home is free to buy the digital technologies each young person wants.

On top of the 'ICT expert' model's problem in reading the market and being slow to make a decision is that it invariably adopts a 'one size fits all' approach, which mandates that every student across every year level in every school will use exactly the same technology, with exactly the same bundle of software. If the 'ICT experts' make a poor choice, all the students in that authority's schools are stuck with that choice. Importantly, so too is the government of the day. The political risk associated with such an approach in such a volatile area is immense.

One thus sees education authorities today still persisting in buying every student in Year 9 to Year 12 in their schools the same low-powered and increasingly dated or near obsolete netbook technology, while the students in their homes acquire and naturally use the latest personal technology of their choice.

Ironically, while the 'ICT experts' and the bureaucrats make much about the savings they can achieve, if the technology they acquire replicates that already in use by the students at home, not only is there the financial folly of the duplication, there is also the waste to taxpayers of having the lesser gear sit unused, rapidly depreciating in value. The educational, financial and, importantly, political risk associated with an education authority acquiring all their students' digital technologies is such as to make it either a brave or quite foolhardy thing to continue to do.

We suggest the wisest way forward for schools, education authorities and governments is to let the market primarily determine each student's desired personal technology. While we appreciate that reading these words will raise some hackles, our suspicion is that until now not many have queried the effectiveness of the current technology selection model. It is wise to reflect on the ever-growing shortcomings of the 'ICT expert' model and the benefits of leaving the choice—as business is increasingly also doing—to the individual user.

THE OPPORTUNITIES

The adoption of a BYOT model not only allows your school to take advantage of the megatrends and the market, but also enables it to capitalise upon the following kind of educational, social development, economic, technical, organisational and political opportunities. As flagged, the hope is that you will continue to identify others, particularly as the understanding of BYOT and its finer workings grows.

Educational

There is the real possibility that in time, with the near total student use of BYOT, apposite teaching, increased awareness, greater personalisation of the teaching and increasingly sophisticated technology, there could be significant improvements secured in various areas of formal learning at various stages in the students' development flowing from the introduction of BYOT. But one needs, as mentioned earlier, to be wary of attributing too much (as has been the case for decades) to one technological development (Ward, Parr & Robinson, 2005).

Most will, as mentioned, focus initially on the impact of BYOT on student learning within the classroom and on the existing curriculum. USA school districts (eSchool News, 2011) are claiming its introduction has already improved student attainment in key learning areas. We find that intriguing in light of the recency of its introduction in those authorities, the fact that students are already using much of the personal technology and that a century of experience (Lee & Winzenried, 2009) has consistently revealed the technology per se has little or no impact on student attainment unless being used by skilled teachers. While not for a moment dismissing the claims, we suggest it is wise to be highly sceptical about any such assertions and look closely at the methodology and the vested interests involved. A host of in- and out-of-school variables impact on each student's learning of a particular attribute. Be wary of the claims that suggest some new magic panacea will suddenly make a difference to student attainment.

That said, the research (Tapscott, 1998; Meredyth et al., 1998; Green & Hannon, 2007; Chowdry, Crawford & Goodman, 2009) and everyday observances have long noted the profound impact that young people's out-of-school use of personal technology has had upon their daily life, play, social interaction, communication, readiness to embrace constant change, the nature of their learning and their increasing facility to teach themselves. BYOT allows each young person to use the technology of their choice, to work with the mobile technologies they find suitable and to decide the medium they will use in creating their work, be it text, image, sound or multimedia.

Each student can moreover normalise the use of their personal suite of digital tools to assist their teaching and learning, anywhere and any time, including now the classroom. Significantly, individual students can use a suite of digital tools they believe appropriate to their particular learning style, which each can in turn personalise. It provides each student with ready 24/7/365 access to their digital office and allows them to organise that office as they choose.

BYOT could in some respects also be titled 'bring your own textbooks'. While the pronounced shift to e-books and electronic variants of school texts and the availability of e-book authoring tools are not restricted to the BYOT model, the students' 24/7/365 use of their own technologies makes it easy for them to move—when they are ready—from the print to the electronic form and accrue the many educational, logistical and financial benefits that flow. Let's hope schools can quickly move away from the immense backpacks even the very young are expected to lug to school and use the smarts and size of the personal technology to relegate the current ergonomic disasters to the history books.

The introduction of BYOT into the school brings with it, consciously or unwittingly, a degree of fusion of in-school and out-of-school teaching and learning. With BYOT, the students will be using in class the personal technology they already use daily at home. They will naturally expect to use it as they always do and to employ the style of self- and peer teaching they prefer (Green & Hannon, 2007). The introduction of that technology and the facility to use it as one wishes does provide an excellent opportunity to form a bridge between the intensive teaching of schools with the far more informal approach used outside. Astute educators can use that bridge to better understand the nature of teaching preferred by young people and its implications for their more holistic 24/7/365 teaching.

Educationally, BYOT introduced astutely could assist to promote a more relevant, attractive and effective learning environment or culture for every young person, both within the school walls and vitally within the wider cyber world, where the students' rights are respected, their voices are heard and their contribution to their own learning is enhanced.

Mobile devices are defining and supporting new communities and their aspirations, attitudes and idioms must be understood and addressed if they are to have parity of access to university education. These transient and mobile communities have their own norms that determine what is acceptable. Such norms might govern etiquette, taste, language, values and ethics, and educators must understand these in order to work effectively within these communities.

Traxler, 2010a, p. 7

As flagged, few educators appear to have appreciated the latter point made by Traxler that since the mid-1990s the young people of the world have developed, embraced and instituted, in conjunction with their peers globally, a mode of teaching and learning appropriate for the networked and digital world. Many of those ways, those mores, as documented by Tapscott (1998), don't accord with the traditional educator's thinking or that of government. While formal schooling is still largely struggling to accommodate the online and digital within the traditional paper-based mode of teaching, young people have from the onset of the Web opted to use a model of teaching and learning relevant to the new context.

The challenge with the introduction of BYOT will be for teachers to understand both teaching environments and to identify how the two can be used to the educational benefit of each student. Central to that quest will be (as Traxler notes) the need to recognise that the out-of-school approach to teaching learning is universally accepted as the norm by young people around the word, is entrenched and will be difficult—if not indeed impossible—for educators to change. The reality is that educators are latecomers whose 'old world' views will continue to be largely rejected.

An important possible adjunct of the increased awareness of out-of-school teaching is the importance of schools to better understand the significant place of peer teaching outside the classroom, the limited use made by students of teachers outside the classroom (Green & Hannon, 2007), the teaching and learning support provided by students' technology and how that understanding might better be used in the classroom. Suzanne Korngold, the Deputy Head of South Forsyth High, for example, has already noted the students' preference for the more collegial approach to learning and desire to work with their peers (Korngold, 2012).

BYOT provides both the opening and the tools for school teaching to finally begin moving from a strongly insular mass-teaching mode to one that is more networked, collaborative and personalised, and which provides students with the opportunity to undertake their teaching and learning when and where they desire. In brief, it enables all your teachers to normalise every use of the networked world. BYOT will in many respects hasten the dismantling of the traditional school walls that separated the in- and out-of-school teaching and learning. The move to a more personalised mode of teaching is important. BYOT finally provides the opportunity to use the approach more extensively with every student. It ensures that each can use their own suite of digital tools everywhere, it allows the teacher to use the approach with all in the group, plus it provides a rare insight into the style of learning preferred by each individual, particularly out of the classroom, and enables all students to self-teach or to learn with their peers.

Interestingly, the case study experience is already revealing that teachers having to work with a mix of technologies are being obliged logistically to leave behind the traditional mass teaching and adopt a significantly more personalised approach. It also opens the way for teachers to reflect on what attributes might better be taught using the technology outside the confines of the classroom. Futurelab (Grant, 2009) research, for example, flags the suggestion that aspects of digital literacy might be more effectively taught in context outside the classroom. Developments like Apple's iBook textbooks not only underscore the inexorable shift to a more personalised approach to teaching, but also a fuller appreciation of the ever-growing facility for self-teaching and, in time, self-assessment.

Approached astutely, with a genuine desire for greater collaboration between the home and the school, BYOT can assist in the development of a more collaborative mode of teaching and facilitate the increased student attainment the research has consistently found where there is close home–school collaboration. Examine any of the following works and you will note the very considerable impact of the collaboration upon the students' academic performance: Grant, 1989; Desforges & Abouchaar, 2003; Hattie, 2009; Berthelsen, 2010.

Allied to this is the impact BYOT can have on the forging of closer, more trusting relationships between the teachers and the students. The current bans on the use of the students' mobile technology and the enforcing of those bans have generated unnecessary angst, particularly at the secondary level. The Deputy Heads of both Forsyth Central High and South Forsyth High commented on the pronounced change in relationships when they not only removed the source of the antipathy, but also began to trust their students.

Introduced astutely, BYOT can (as Bailey Mitchell [2012] observed) be a highly exciting, game-changing educational development embraced by the students, teachers and parents alike. What impressed the authors with so many of the case study schools was the excitement, energy and pride in what was being achieved, seeing how enthused the students were and the impact the development was already having on key learning factors like attractiveness, student attendance and interest in the learning.

Schools' and societies' adoption of the BYOT model and the appreciation that in a networked world young people learn 24/7/365 might finally prompt education and educational certification authorities to recognise that teaching, learning and student assessment in a networked world should not be restricted to that occurring within a physical place called school.

Social

The adoption of BYOT and the multifaceted use of students' personal technology signal to all a fact well understood by wider society, but seemingly less so by some educators, that the digital now plays a central role in the social development and education of the world's young people, and as such needs to be far better understood and perhaps better taken on board by our teachers and indeed all of the nation's educators. One senses that at times some educators would prefer that the students' distinct and all-pervasive use of the digital is best left outside the classroom. However, the moment your school opens its doors to BYOT, there needs to be a better understanding of this all-pervasive use and how it can be meshed with the school's teaching and learning.

Cassell & Cramer's (2008) research, for example, on the key role that personal technology plays in the social and indeed the sexual development of teenage girls should be understood by all secondary school educators about to experience BYOT. The following observation should be appreciated by all.

Historical evidence demonstrates that women and young people have long appropriated technology to their own ends in culturally important ways, but that very appropriation has proved a danger to the established social order, and by proxy has diminished in particular the female users in the eyes of those around them; has rendered them, in fact, 'a threat to societal values and interests'.

Cassell & Cramer, 2008, p. 62

Teachers should also be aware of the analysis by Ito and her team (2008) of young people's everyday use of the digital, the different categories of user and the teaching implications that flow once the school opts to use that technology.

Significantly, BYOT ought to enable the school and its students to take advantage of the bridge mentioned earlier and work collaboratively on the students' social, personal-development and emotional skills within a networked world. The technology in class can, for example, be used to facilitate the students' use of their own synchronised suite of digital technologies to better, and more effectively and efficiently, plan and organise their own learning and lives, or assist them in acquiring the skills to contextualise the appropriate use of their suite of digital technologies—a vital element of the modern workforce.

Your school's adoption of BYOT should assist in breaking down the strong home–school digital divide that exists in many situations and the sense that the school is out of touch with the everyday networked and digital world.

Economic

As discussed earlier, the normalised use of BYOT allows schools to employ a predominantly market-based school personal technology resourcing model that can be readily sustained over the long haul and which allows the school to remain current with the technology without risk, in an era of rapid, often uncertain technological change—and often limited technological expertise. When schools go digital, when the students', teachers' and parents' expectations grow at pace, when key technological developments happen within months and the finite life cycle of every piece of technology gets ever shorter, it is economically challenging as well as politically risky to leave the choice of the personal technology solely to 'ICT experts'.

A market-based BYOT personal technology model—where each family decides what technology, hardware and software to acquire and when, and when to update that technology—removes the financial and political risk from government and the considerable waste universally associated with 'one size fits all' personal technology schemes that see the technology sitting idle or underused for a significant proportion of its relatively short life. The scheme also enables the vast majority of the technology used within a networked school community to be used every minute of the year, in marked contrast to the pattern of old where much of the digital technology was locked away in the school and used only between 9 am and 3 pm for a limited number of days each year.

Most importantly, it removes the waste associated with the family and the government both buying the same mobile technology and one of the items sitting unused—sheer folly. Lee flagged this pitfall some 15 years ago (Lee, 1996), but until recently schools and education authorities have paid no regard to the wise use of public monies or investigated the extent or nature of the senseless replication of hardware and software acquisition. If only a 50 per cent replication, that itself represented a gross waste of public funds.

BYOT potentially provides your school with significant recurrent educational resources, which allows it to redeploy its scarce resources to other operations. It is vital that the school leadership view the BYOT contribution not simply as a financial contribution but part of a wider contribution by the homes to the resourcing and development of the school.

The degree of recurrent savings for the school—and in turn the government—will depend (as discussed more fully in Chapter 8) on variables like the model of BYOT chosen, teacher readiness to use the students' technology, the rate at which the students opt for BYOT, the money to be spent upgrading infrastructure and the efficiencies derived from the astute whole-school operation's use of the students' technology. It will also depend on the extent to which the school, and possibly the school in conjunction with its local authority, has moved from its reliance on paper to a digital operational base. The financial savings possible in many education authorities from simply moving from hardcopy textbooks and their storage to digital variants could be considerable. Similarly, the shift to near total digitally based operations allows schools and their education authorities to achieve efficiencies, a degree of integration and a level of synergy unachievable in a paper-based operation.

As we explore more fully in Chapter 9, it is likely that in time significant recurrent savings could be made in:

- the acquisition of personal (desktop and mobile) technology
- software licences and apps
- maintenance and support of student technologies
- enhanced efficiencies in school administration, organisation and communications
- reduced use of paper, textbooks, hardcopy library books and printing and copying technology

It is appreciated that part of those savings will likely need to be redeployed on bolstering the infrastructure and wireless access, and in particular in acquiring extra bandwidth. In time, BYOT would obviate the need for local and national governments to outlay the considerable funds needed regularly to update students' personal digital technology and to administer the implementation of such rollouts.

Today, in a sizeable part of the developed world where the GFC is still impacting and school financial cutbacks abound, an astutely implemented BYOT where the homes and the schools collaborate closely might be one of the few ways schools will be able to work with the current digital technology. Economically it allows each school community to plan with certainty, to plan more efficiently and effectively and to largely remove its reliance on often uncertain government technology budgets and the 'ICT experts' within the education authority bureaucracies. It enables each school to invest astutely in longer-term major infrastructure upgrades and maintenance—and largely move away from the hassles, inefficiencies and expenses associated with the short life of personal digital technology.

BYOT says to government and school leaders that in an ever-more networked world the parents and students have a key economic role to play, and as such their contribution needs to be factored into any school development strategy. In Australia, the national government is already unwittingly supporting the move to BYOT with its annual student technology tax incentive.

Technological

Your school's adoption of BYOT, coupled with the school's level of recurrent funding, will likely oblige it to fundamentally re-examine its digital operations, the role the 'ICT team' should play, its fit with the school's shaping educational vision and development path, the services that should be provided, its budgeting, its staffing and the relationship with the other teaching staff, the students and students' homes. It will be a time to refocus its operations. Gone overnight will be its 'stand-alone' operations where the 'ICT team' largely decided unilaterally on the technological arrangements for the school. In brief, in moving to a model of BYOT, the school will leave behind the now traditional school technology support model and move to one that is fundamentally different in purpose and nature.

There will be implications. In some situations you could be looking at reducing the level of ICT support staffing, either at the school or via the subcontractors. BYOT should allow the school to focus on the less changeable infrastructure and largely remove the more volatile and risky personal technology operations from its brief.

Organisation and communication

BYOT provides the opportunity for each student to organise their learning and school activities on their own digital tools, to synchronise those entries on all their equipment and do away with the cost and inefficiencies of paper diaries and organisers.

With each student having their own digital technology, the way is opened to move to a near-total digital administration, a strongly personalised and integrated organisational and communications schema rendering obsolete many of the traditional mass paper communications and organisational operations, and in so doing to reap the increases in efficiency, effectiveness and synergy. As the case studies already reveal, the facility for even small schools to make significant ongoing savings and redeploy those staff is considerable.

Political

Politically, BYOT provides politicians and governments with that rare opportunity to:

- meet their constituents' wishes re the recognition and use of their own technology in schooling, while at the same time assisting to enhance the relevance and attraction of the schooling
- enrich the resources available to schools while saving the government potentially considerable long-term recurrent funds, particularly at a time in most electorates where significant savings have to be made
- foster greater home–school collaboration in schooling and underscore the vital educational role the home should play in a networked world.

BYOT says to politicians that the parents are prepared to make a significant contribution to their children's teaching, but in return they will want greater recognition and voice in that schooling. It also potentially removes government from not only much of the significant cost of funding the upgrade of personal technology but also the considerable and growing risk associated with getting that upgrade wrong.

The home commitment opens the way for the community to have a more significant voice in schooling, fitting well with the moves to deploy greater autonomy to school communities. Very importantly, BYOT affords governments the opportunity to move positively away from the 'free' school-funding model of the 1870s to one that is a mix of public, private and community.

THE BANDWAGON

The last but by no means least of the factors that will eventually impel schools in the developed world to employ some type of BYOT model will be the 'BYOT bandwagon'—that seemingly inevitable desire to keep up with the Joneses. As mentioned earlier, in undertaking our research we were surprised by the magnitude of the tsunami on the horizon and the number of schools and education authorities intending to make the move in the near future. As happened in the USA, the UK and Australia, as soon as there are schools that have 'successfully' introduced the model, the pressure will grow on all the others to join the bandwagon.

Let us be clear: we are not suggesting this should be a reason for making the move; it is simply a reality that in conjunction with all the aforementioned factors will eventually impel all schools to move. A word of warning, if yours is a leadership that appears to want to join the bandwagon, do alert them to the holistic nature of the development, the imperative of addressing the readiness factors discussed in the next chapter and employing an astute implementation strategy.

CONCLUSION

In reality, BYOT is a natural consequence of societies'—and in turn, schooling's—move to a networked world. However, there is a big step between understanding the forces at play and the opportunities available and moving your school to the position where it can take advantage of those openings. Virtually all are dependent on 100 per cent of students using BYOT.

As you reflect on the analysis in the following chapters of what is entailed in achieving that sustained 100 per cent student usage, you will better understand the amount of work and leadership required for the school to reap most of the desired outcomes, and how easy it is for poorly led schools to not realise all the potential benefits.

....

FORSYTH COUNTY SCHOOL DISTRICT

Situation

Forsyth County School District constitutes part of metropolitan Atlanta, Georgia, USA.

An urban growth area, the district is one of the wealthiest in Georgia, with many of its parents working in Atlanta.

Forsyth County has been to the fore in the use of instructional technology in schools for some time and was one of the first districts in the USA to introduce interactive whiteboards throughout its classrooms. In the mid-2000s, the County's instructional leadership recognised the need to move away from the common 'one size fits all' Microsoft model and gradually install the infrastructure that would enable all the schools to make far greater use of the emerging digital technology in the personalisation of teaching and learning and the collaboration with the homes.

By 2010, it was apparent many of the schools in the County had normalised the use of the digital across the school, forged closer links with the students' homes and recognised the folly and unnecessary angst created by forbidding the use of students' personal technology. Unwittingly, Forsyth County was naturally evolving a model of BYOT.

As Jill Hobson, the Director of Instructional Technology, noted the district didn't have a great plan to move to BYOT, it evolved. That said, it evolved because an astute education authority leadership team had the acumen and vision to see the way forward, to recognise the kind of twenty-first century education the district should provide, to identify the infrastructure and the support the teachers would require, and they had the willingness to let each school adopt an approach that would suit its context.

They were shaping the future direction of schooling. In researching the introduction of BYOT we struggled to find a comparable leadership group. Most central office instructional technology units were more concerned about protecting their power base than facilitating the appropriate education.

For fuller details refer to: http://www.forsyth.k12.ga.us/.
Contacts: Jill Hobson, Director of Instructional Technology
Bailey Mitchell, Chief Technology and Information Officer
Tim Clark, District Instructional Technology Specialist

BYOT developments

Fundamental to the development of BYOT in Forsyth County is a culture that rewards change, a desire to let each school's leadership adopt an appropriate way forward and a comprehensive backup strategy that supports each school's efforts and ensures it is consonant with the County's desires. Little wonder the County is showing the way forward globally.

It bears stressing that the Forsyth approach is in marked contrast to many other USA education authorities introducing BYOT that continue to use a top-down, control-over, 'one size fits all' model.

Forsyth County is approaching the development of BYOT from a networked operational mindset, promoting the value of the teachers in their schools supporting themselves but also coming together at the District level to support their other colleagues. Additionally, it places considerable store in the feedback of the students and their families.

Importantly, the District team continues to set the direction and provide infrastructure that can accommodate the growing traffic that will flow from total student BYOT uptake. See http://www.forsyth.k12.ga.us/page/824.

It is thus not surprising to note that the bus tours that were originally intended to educate the District's teachers are now being patronised by teachers from interstate and overseas.

CHAPTER **4**

CONTEXT AND READINESS

Readying your school for BYOT is crucial for the sustained success of any BYOT initiative. Yet the current literature makes no mention of readiness or of developing an approach suited to your context, seemingly forgetting that every school and its community is unique. The assumption is that whenever they decide, any school or education authority can introduce a model of BYOT with no or minimal preparation.

They can—but there is a considerable likelihood of failure or very limited success that goes nowhere near realising the kind of potential described in the previous chapter. In one of the notable case studies, School A, the paucity of the school's preparation led it into a Balkan-like war among the staff. The plan should be to ready your particular school's base for a smooth and successful implementation, sustained development and speedy movement to a phase where the model is normalised and becomes near invisible.

What we are seeking to do below is to provide you with an ideal scenario. However, we are very conscious that invariably one cannot always make the move in ideal conditions and that often (as the likes of The Illawarra Grammar example attests) leaders have to make the call to move forward in less than ideal circumstances, fully aware of the risks involved.

CONTEXT

The commonness of less-than-ideal situations is one of the reasons why we wish to underscore a reality often forgotten by central bureaucrats and politicians: that every school is a unique entity with its own specific context. As a consequence, the BYOT model you opt for at a particular point in the school's evolution could rightly be significantly different to that of a school up the road.

Every school, even within the most centralised of education systems, has a distinct:

- setting and clientele, with its own community, ever-evolving networks, socioeconomic circumstances and community resourcing and support
- governance structure and degree of autonomy
- shaping educational vision
- developmental strategy
- principal, with their own leadership style, with no two ever being the same
- ever-changing mix of staff
- organisational structures, culture and ways of doing things
- manner and level of collaboration with its homes.

Significantly, in some situations schools might also have a different curriculum. We are working on the assumption that the digital technology is used in every area of learning from the start of school onwards and is not restricted to a specific subject or area of learning.

That said, we recognise that a few countries, like the UK, have opted to focus the development of the digital in a separate subject in the secondary years called 'ICT', a move that invariably leads to a lesser use of the digital in the other subjects. That impact is evidenced in the last of the Becta annual reports (Becta, 2009a), where the use of the digital in core secondary subjects remained very low. Such an approach might explain why schools in some more affluent nations have been that little bit slower to move to a model of BYOT.

Vitally, every school is at a different point along the evolutionary road. Some are still very much paper-based while others, often within the same authority, are operating within a networked paradigm.

As you examine the key readiness variables below and apply them to your school, you will appreciate the very considerable danger (dare we say, the folly) in education authorities mandating a strict 'one size fits all' adoption of BYOT by all its schools. The inadvisability of such a philosophy is amplified when applied to a situation in which the school or authority is seeking to have the homes volunteer the use of their personal technology.

READINESS

While well aware that BYOT is still at a nascent point in its development, we have tried to identify key areas you will need to prepare in order to give your school the desired base on which to build. Use it as a checklist, and be quite blunt in your analysis when evaluating where your school is at with each of the preconditions. You will rapidly appreciate that your greatest challenge will be human; by comparison, the technical aspect will be simple. Get the foundations right from the outset and it is more likely that BYOT will in time become a normalised everyday part of the school's operations.

We have identified five, possibly six, key readiness factors:
- Normalised use of the digital
- Genuine home–school collaboration
- Principal's leadership
- Appropriate infrastructure
- Champions
- Education authority (if applicable).

Normalised use of the digital

If your school is to achieve 100 per cent student uptake of BYOT and in turn normalise the use of the students' technology, all the key members of the school's community—its students, parents and teachers—have to have and be using the technology. In particular, every teacher has to have normalised the use of the digital in their everyday teaching. The research (Lee & Finger, 2010) indicates that it is not enough for the teachers to normalise the use outside the classroom; it has to be in the teaching.

Teachers

It is hard to stress how vital total teacher usage is. The bottom line is that if a teacher does not use the digital as a normal facet of their everyday teaching, neither will the students. At this stage in the evolution of schooling and the movement from a paper-based model of teaching to one that is predominantly digitally based, the 'missing element' in most schools is the teacher.

There are three vital questions you need to ask upfront of your school.
- What percentage of the teachers is provided with a personal digital device or the funds to acquire such a device by their employer?

- What percentage of the teachers has normalised the use of the digital in their everyday teaching?
- If it is not 100 per cent, why not? And—as a side question—what is the school leadership doing to remedy the situation?

The ideal, which some of the case study schools have achieved, is for all teachers to have normalised the use of the digital in their everyday teaching, understanding the educational benefit of collaborating with the students' homes, and being willing and able to collaborate. That position will not be reached overnight. As Lee and Winzenried (2009, p. 225) demonstrate, striving for that ideal entails the school successfully and simultaneously addressing the following nine human and technological variables:

- Teacher acceptance
- Working with the givens
- Teacher training and teacher developmental support
- Nature and availability of the technology
- Appropriate content/software
- Infrastructure
- Finance
- School and education authority leadership
- Implementation.

A fuller consideration of what is entailed in total teacher digital take-off can be found in Lee and Winzenried's *The use of instructional technology in schools* (2009) and in a shorter article at http://www.malleehome.com.

The schools operating within the digital and, in particular, the networked mode will have addressed all of these variables. A key factor is that every teacher has their own personal digital technology, provided ideally (as it is in New Zealand) by the teacher's employer.

Recent work on the Australian scene has revealed an utter hodge-podge of somewhere between 40 and 50 per cent of teachers in the state, Catholic and independent schools at the beginning of 2012 still not having been provided with this most basic of tools by their employer. (We say in the region of 40–50 per cent because no comprehensive study has been conducted, even at a time when the national and state governments were rolling out a national 1:1 laptop program for all students in Year 9 to Year 12.) It is appreciated that the percentage of teachers in Australia using a personal digital device will be higher because a significant but as yet unknown percentage buy their own technology or acquire it through a salary sacrifice model.

The authors would suggest that in providing all the teachers with their digital tools, employers adopt many of the core attributes of the BYOT model, provide the staff with an appropriate allowance and let each secure their preferred technology. The top-down, 'one size fits all' model that alienates the young also peeves the teachers.

In contemplating a move to BYOT, you will want to have at least a critical mass of the school's teachers—that is, 70–80 per cent—having normalised the in-class use of the digital. To achieve 100 per cent student uptake of BYOT in the primary or elementary schools you must have all of the teachers using the digital naturally in class. At the secondary level, the total uptake can be achieved with a slightly lower percentage. You can commence the move to BYOT well short of that figure, but it entails a risk.

Along the way you will also need to know what percentage of your teachers is using a teaching style that encourages the students to bring their digital tools to class. The importance of this finding will become ever clearer. The case studies are reaffirming that young people, even at the primary school level, are very astute and if their teacher doesn't use a more student-centred type of teaching that encourages the use of the digital technology, the students won't bring their tools to that class. You can well appreciate why. While this issue will not prevent a school introducing a model of BYOT, it is a factor that will likely stop the 100 per cent uptake.

Interestingly, in our research we learnt of 'elite' schools—public and independent—that were intending to inform parents what mobile technology they would have to purchase for their children's use at school. Given the importance certain parents attach to their children attending such a school, it is highly likely that this top-down model will result in the total acquisition of the technology. The challenge facing these schools will be all the teachers using a mode of digitally based teaching that has the students using their technology in class. There is the very real chance of the student technology becoming wasted window-dressing. The assertion has been made that the student use will oblige the teachers to change their ways. The authors know of no research that supports that strategy. We are, however, aware of years of experience and research (Cuban, 1986; Lee and Winzenried, 2009) that show that teachers as the gatekeepers to their own classrooms will not use a technology in their teaching if they don't believe it will assist the students' learning.

A special mention does need to be made of the readiness of a subgroup of the staff, the ICT team. The operations of your ICT team (as suggested in Chapter 3) could be markedly impacted by the adoption of a mode of BYOT. Some ICT teams keen to ensure that they are supporting the shaping educational vision of the school will embrace, and may in fact champion, its introduction—as is evidenced in the Broulee, Kolbe College and Manor Lakes case studies. Other ICT teams happy with their control over every aspect of the school's technology may well resent the mere suggestion of the idea—as in the case of School A. They will perceive it as a threat to their power.

The school or education authority leadership should be able to turn to its technology specialists to provide the requisite expert advice and to flag the changes required to make best use of BYOT. You will need to decide if your ICT team is ready to provide this advice. It is simply a case of you reading the lie of the land and, knowing the people involved, deciding how best to approach the group or to work around them.

Parents

An underlying assumption when introducing a model of BYOT is that all the students' homes have internet access and that the parents have normalised the everyday use of the digital and will in the main soon be convinced of the educational worth of collaborating with the school in adopting a BYOT approach. It is a good idea to check.

If your school has not in the parents' eyes genuinely collaborated with them in the past, it will have to prove its genuine desire to collaborate before a number of parents will allow their technology to be used, and that will take time and action. Bear in mind you could well have a significant number of parents still highly alienated with schooling who are very reluctant to even set foot in the school, let alone allow their technology to be used in the classroom.

You will need to work on securing the support of all your parents.

Students

Based on a plethora of research (Green & Hannon, 2007; ACMA, 2007; Tapscott, 2009) we are assuming that the students have normalised the everyday use of the digital and are thinking within the networked mode where collaboration is the norm, and as such will be ready to collaborate in mounting a model of BYOT. The case study experience reinforces that belief.

As indicated, whether or not they opt to take that technology to class will largely depend on the authenticity of the school's desire to collaborate with them, and the teacher making it worthwhile.

Home–school collaboration

Authentic collaboration by the school with the home and respect for the contribution that can be made by the parents (and often the grandparents) and the students themselves are fundamental to taking best advantage of the vast majority of the opportunities identified in Chapter 3. Its centrality will become ever-more apparent in your journey and thus it is imperative that you regard BYOT as a form of home–school collaboration.

From a parent's perspective, how would you rate your school's collaboration with the vast majority of your homes, where 1 is very poor, 2 poor, 3 average, 4 good and 5 very good?
        1--------2--------3--------4--------5

Use your answers to this question to determine how ready your school is to genuinely collaborate with its homes in introducing a model of BYOT.

Principal

Every one of the case studies has (not surprisingly) affirmed in both a positive and a negative way the importance of the principal in the successful whole-school introduction of BYOT. Without that leadership from the top the school will struggle.

Each case study affirms the importance of having school leaders who understand the myriad of ever-evolving interrelated variables to be simultaneously addressed in developing a school operating in the networked mode, who appreciate how a development like BYOT has to be seamlessly integrated into the everyday operations of the school and who have the courage to lead in unchartered territory. In many of the situations, such as at Noadswood, Illawarra Grammar, Manor Lakes and Broulee, that high level of leadership is provided not only by the principal but also by other members of the executive.

Mention was made earlier of the 2010 USA survey (Project Tomorrow, 2011; 2012) that revealed 65 per cent of principals said 'no way' to the idea of allowing student-owned digital technology in 'their' school. The indicators suggest that kind of thinking will be found at the primary and secondary level across the developed world. We are prepared to go out on a limb and suggest that the 65 per cent of principals are in schools that have yet to normalise the total school use of the digital. That said, there are very few school principals who are not committed to doing the utmost for all their students. That has invariably been their mission in life.

Your job will be to convince your head how BYOT, in line with the reasoning discussed in Chapter 3, can enhance the overall education of every child. Remember, the school principal, as the CEO of the school, is the person who will ultimately decide when your school will move to a model of BYOT. That is why they need to be ready or readied.

Being brutally blunt: do you have any chance of winning the support of your principal or won't you know until you have done your homework?

Infrastructure

There are three key elements you need to check with regard to infrastructure.

The first is the obvious one: the school, classroom and teacher technology.

The second is far less obvious. If you take your mind back to many of the opportunities flagged in Chapter 3, they all presume the school will have an appropriate digital communications suite that will allow the total school community to communicate digitally. It will use much of the same technical infrastructure as the first, but will also include a suite of specialist communications software and facilities.

The third, which is even less obvious, is the school's readiness to astutely manage the ever-growing body of digital resources that will be used and created by the students and the teachers. Whether yours is an iCentre, resource centre or library, you will need the wherewithal and the leadership required to expertly manage the emerging e-books, e-texts, digital teaching resources and student creations.

Teaching infrastructure

While we go into the teaching infrastructure in far greater depth in Chapter 7, in brief:

- Every teaching room should have an appropriate core suite of digital instructional technologies to allow every teacher to normalise the use of the digital in their teaching in that room. If the teaching technology is restricted to computer labs, you will have major readiness issues until you have at least whole-class digital presentation technology, an IWB or data projector and access to the internet in every teaching room.
- Every teacher has to have their own computer and probably their own personal digital device. Depending on the personal technology the students opt to bring to class, the school might need to provide (in addition to a laptop) some or all of the teachers with an allowance—or the gear itself—that will enable them to also have a mobile device consonant with that used by most of the students. For example, if the students opt in large numbers to use iPod touches and that device's functionality is not understood by the teachers, support needs to be provided.
- There should be high-speed wi-fi 'anywhere, any time' infrastructure across the campus, with capacity to accommodate ever-increasing use. From a security perspective, there is much to be said for this network to be separate from the school administration network.
- There should be available supplementary technology/support to assist phased uptake of BYOT. Do you have the personal digital technology in each room that will allow the school to look after 'those without' while BYOT is being phased in?

As one of our case studies demonstrates, if the plan isn't to phase out the school acquisition of personal technology while phasing in BYOT, you are well on course for a major power play or even a brawl.

On a scale of 1 to 5, where 1 is very poor, 3 is sound and 5 is very good or exceptional, how would you rate the readiness of the school's 'teaching infrastructure'?
1--------2--------3--------4--------5

If you don't rate it as at least 4, you have some major readiness issues as both the students and teachers ought to expect automatic digital usage and internet access 100 per cent of the teaching time.

Digital communications suite

The school will want a tightly integrated, multifaceted, multiway digital communications suite. It should be built around an integrating website, providing personalised email communication with all within the school's community and a complementary set of social networking facilities that allows it to take full advantage of the efficiencies—economies, productivity and ultimately the synergies possible in a digital world, and in particular the students' personal technology.

On a scale of 1 to 5, where 1 is very poor, 3 is sound and 5 is very good or exceptional, how would you rate the readiness of the school's digital communication's suite?

    1--------2--------3--------4--------5

Management of digital resources

The current state of play in this area requires you to have someone on top of their game able to handle it.

Although much media hype is being generated about e-books, electronic texts, great online offerings and the quality of the interactive multimedia teaching materials, the reality is that the digital publishers and resellers, including Apple and Google, are still largely approaching schooling from the traditional insular schooling paradigm, with most having yet to come to grips with a development like BYOT. Their prime concern is how to make the biggest possible profit in an ever-evolving scene.

It is thus imperative that you have in the position a person or team capable of leading the school through very dangerous territory, meeting the school's digital resource requirements without committing the school to expensive, rapidly dated arrangements while at the same time having a system to manage the digital resources while the industry gets its act together. Information management systems and e-book resellers attuned to the new scene need to be carefully selected.

On a scale of 1 to 5, where 1 is very poor, 3 is sound and 5 is very good or exceptional, how would you rate the readiness of the school's current personnel to manage the digital resources?

    1--------2--------3--------4--------5

This is a situation where if the existing personnel cannot soon be brought up to speed, staff changes might be required.

Champions

Interestingly, all the case studies have had their champion(s) promoting the move. While it is admittedly a relatively small sample, this finding is wholly consistent with the organisational change literature.

In brief, your school will need a champion, or preferably a team of champions, guiding the move to BYOT. Sometimes in the case studies it was the principal, an assistant principal, a director of information services, a head of technology or a committed teacher—but regardless of who it is, your school will need that champion to shape the initiative. You will need 'doers' and it really does not matter what formal position they occupy, or indeed if it is a parent, student or member of the school's community playing the role.

Education authority (if applicable)

The ideal is to have a local education authority—like that of Forsyth County—that works with all its schools in the introduction of BYOT and provides the requisite direction, infrastructure, support and training. However, it is already clear there will be significant variability in the outlook of education authorities towards 'their' schools using a BYOT model. While the likes of Forsyth County, the Tasmanian and Victorian departments of education and the Parramatta Catholic Education Office are already assisting interested schools by helping with the campus wi-fi and student network access, others have central office ICT teams doing their utmost to maintain the present 'one size fits all' approach.

You will need to check your authority's readiness. Importantly, you will also want your principal to check the scene.

Most in leadership positions in education authorities can read the megatrends, appreciate the advantages of the market and understand the considerable educational, economic, organisational and political benefits of BYOT, particularly at a time when many are obliged to make significant financial savings and to encourage greater school autonomy. But there will be those, particularly those associated with the technology, who could be reluctant to cede any power.

Of note are the schools in the case studies that have been able to make the move, even when the education authority's ICT unit opposed the move.

Your school

Bearing in mind the abovementioned readiness factors and your call on where your school is at with each, where would you position your school on this evolutionary five-scale (as described below)?

1--------2--------3--------4--------5

1   **Paper based:** where the majority of your teachers are using in the main paper, pens and the teaching board—be it black, green or white—in their everyday teaching. (Of note, this was still the norm in the vast majority of classrooms in the OECD in 2009 [Lee & Winzenried, 2009].)

2   **Early digital:** where 60–70 per cent of your teachers are using the digital in their everyday teaching, and as such nearing the 'critical mass' stage and 'digital take-off' (Lee & Gaffney, 2008)

3   **Digital:** where all the teaching staff have normalised the use of the digital in their everyday teaching, but where the school is still operating as a discrete, 'stand-alone' entity primarily within the traditional school walls

4   **Early networked:** where the staff have normalised the use of the digital in their everyday teaching and are beginning to use the networks to operate outside the school walls and the normal school hours, and starting to 'teach' more collaboratively with the students and their homes—educationally and/or administratively—and the wider networked community (Lee & Finger, 2010)

5   **Networked:** where the staff have normalised the use of the digital in their everyday teaching and are collaborating authentically with all the parties inside and outside the school—professional and non-professional—in the 24/7/365 teaching of young people.

CONCLUSION

Your reading of the school's readiness should then inform the school's development strategy and elicit the type and extent of change and remedying required before you adopt your initial BYOT model and move to the implementation stage.

KOLBE CATHOLIC COLLEGE

Situation

- Kolbe Catholic College is a relatively new Year 7–12 coeducational school situated on the coast in a new growth area south of Perth, Western Australia (WA).
- The school is part of the Perth Catholic education system and as such has considerable autonomy in its selection of staff and the allocation of its resources.
- It has approximately 1000 students, with the college socioeconomic profile sitting on the Australian norm.
- In the last decade under the principalship of Caroline Payne and more recently Robyn Miller, the school has established a reputation as one of Australia's leaders in the use of technology in teaching and learning.

Fuller details on the college can be found at: http://www.kolbe.wa.edu.au/.
Contact: Bradley Tyrell, Head of Digital Technology

BYOT developments

Like many of the other case studies, Kolbe College is one of the first in its region to move to a model of BYOT. Again like other case studies, the move to BYOT flowed naturally from the school's normalised use of the digital and making far better use of the students' personal technology.

The school was well equipped technology-wise, running a 1:1 Windows-based computing program, having all teaching rooms with the appropriate technology, with all staff being provided with laptops and a critical mass of teachers using the digital in their teaching.

Conscious of the students' desire to use their own technology and the recognition that the school could not sustain the present 1:1 laptop program once the national project ceased, it gradually moved to allow the students to begin bringing their own technology in 2011.

CHAPTER **5**

THE MODEL AND THE OPTIONS

Now you are rapidly moving from the theoretical to the practical and need to make a decision critical to the effective introduction of BYOT. The realisation of the opportunities outlined earlier requires that you adopt a BYOT package in harmony with your school's shaping educational vision, one that is consistent and readily integrated with the school's overall developmental strategy and appropriate to where your school is at in its evolution and readiness to collaborate with its homes.

Equally important is a package that facilitates the realisation of the desired outcomes and encourages all students to actually use their own digital technology in the classroom. Grab any old package (as sadly some of the more naive are doing) or an inappropriate package and there is a real likelihood that the school won't reach the desired 100 per cent sustained usage. Don't assume that by simply adopting BYOT the students and their families will flock to bring their technology into the classroom. The choice of the appropriate package is crucial.

The options open to you are extensive and the facility for error immense. What we have tried to do below is to build on the experiences of the case study schools and examine the major options with a view to enabling you to adopt the appropriate package.

We have taken as a given a base model of BYOT that incorporates the core elements identified in the earlier definition, and in so doing have omitted the pseudo forms of BYOT. Also, not unlike choosing a car, one can add any number of options to the base model to create the desired deluxe model variations.

As with a car, money—particularly that within your homes—will influence your choices, but so too will be the school's readiness for BYOT and the extent to which the school is willing to collaborate with and trust its clients. Trust in the students is emerging as a crucial variable.

It may well be that circumstances will dictate that you start with a package knowing full well some parts are inappropriate and are likely to fail, but hopefully out of that failure will come an appreciation by all of the better way forward. In commenting on the options, we recognise that we are at an early stage in the evolution of BYOT and that as the understanding of the development grows, so too will the options.

TRANSITIONING

We are working on the assumption that like all the most astute case studies, schools will transition into BYOT with a view to achieving total student usage as soon as is feasible and desired. It is most assuredly not a black-and-white case of saying 'on day X this approach ends and BYOT starts the next day'. Indeed one may well be talking a year or two, even when the school has normalised the use of the digital and its community has endorsed the concept and employed an astute implementation strategy. (And if done not so well, it will take appreciably longer.)

One needs to ready oneself mentally for that kind of time frame. The case study situation makes it clear that many schools will be transitioning from a model where they have been funding every student's ready access to the technology, such as via 1:1 computing, and thus have time to make the transition before acquiring any new personal technology. Importantly, those schools also have some time to let BYOT evolve.

What is also evident from the case study experience is that the school principal does need to make it clear from the outset that the old will be phased out and BYOT phased in. You cannot afford to have two competing technology resourcing models in conflict with the associated competing power blocs.

You'll be aware of the many variables in your situation that will determine the nature, timing and approximate longevity of your transition. Clearly the readiness factors discussed in Chapter 4 will have a major bearing, but so too will factors such as when technology leases expire, whether you are going to use a pilot approach or indeed wish to wait for a significant technological upgrade.

Brainstorm the factors that need to be borne in mind and address them when selecting the desired BYOT package and shaping your implementation strategy.

THE OPTIONS

The various options in considering your school's BYOT model are summarised in Table 5.1. In considering the options, it bears remembering the following points.

1   You are going to have to entice a very knowledgeable and discerning clientele to use their digital technology in class, to use the school's secure wi-fi network and to ask them to possibly enter into a usage agreement with the school. You need to attract their patronage. Any perceived impediments at the beginning or during the operation of BYOT will likely detract from that quest.

2   The students, perhaps unwittingly, are in a position of strength, with the majority having ready 24/7/365 internet access and, as such, do not have to rely on the school's network for access. Most could opt to bypass the school's network if the restrictions imposed are perceived to be unreasonable.

3   Increasingly, parents and students will expect to be genuinely consulted in the operation and refinement of BYOT.

Some observations

In relation to the various options as outlined in Table 5.1, below are some observations flowing from the case study analysis that are worth noting.

Option 1

All the case study schools have researched the home internet access situation with each student and sought—as best they could—to support those students without the requisite technology at home. As an option, you could choose not to offer any support, but you do open the school to strong criticism in relation to equity.

As we've made clear, the authors are strongly of the view that no student in the school should be disadvantaged when it comes to technology access. Moreover, we are increasingly of the view that the

Table 5.1 *The options*

NUMBER	HOME/STUDENT RESPONSIBILITIES	SCHOOL RESPONSIBILITIES
1	Home internet access	Caters for disadvantaged
2a	Selects and acquires suite of personal digital technologies	• Promotes tax/government technology incentives for families with school children • Accepts student's choice of digital technology
2b	Selects and acquires suite of any personal digital technologies	• Promotes tax/government technology incentives for families with school children • Advises on technology requirements, but accepts student's choice
3	Students bring to class personal mobile technology	Provides every teaching room with appropriate suite of whole-class digital instructional technology with internet access
4a	Pays for desired personal telecommunications connection	Provides free and protected campus-wide wi-fi access for all students via agreed log-on
4b	Provides desired personal telecommunications	Provides campus-wide protected wi-fi access for all students at a charge
5a	Collaborates with school in identifying in-school usage arrangements	Implements the suite of usage arrangements decided in collaboration with the homes
5b		School/education authority mandates the student's personal technology usage arrangements
5c		Puts nothing on paper, at least initially. Trusts students. Lets BYOT evolve naturally
6a	Home provides personal applications software/apps	Provides desired supplementary software applications/apps
6b	Home provides personal applications software/apps	Students expected to provide desired common supplementary educational software applications/apps
7	Students responsible for storage of personal digital data	Wi-fi access to digital storage for student educational work
8a	Students responsible for care and maintenance of own technology	• Provides secure personal storage facility for each student • Deals with any in-school theft of student technology • Takes responsibility for the maintenance of student technology

⟶

Table 5.1 *(continued)*

NUMBER	HOME/STUDENT RESPONSIBILITIES	SCHOOL RESPONSIBILITIES
8b	Students responsible for care and maintenance of own technology	• School provides secure personal storage facility for each student • School deals with any in-school theft of student technology • Takes no responsibility for the maintenance of student technology
9	Students provide own desired suite of interactive multimedia creation tools	Provides supplementary technology
10	Students provide personal digital communications, allowing school to communicate with them anywhere, any time	Provides digital communications suite
11	Students primarily responsible for ongoing 24/7/365 enhancement of digital fluency	• Collaborates with students and parents in enhancing each student's digital fluency • Monitors and reports diagnostically upon each student's development
12	Students upgrade/expand their suite of personal technology when they wish, strongly impacted by the market	Remains alert to accommodating state-of-the-art personal digital technology

individual school is best placed to ensure each of its students has use of the requisite technology. As we elaborate in Chapter 8, the funding or actual resources can be provided by the school itself, the local education authority, the national government or some other body, but it should be the school that ensures each student is provided the required technology and support.

Thus far, such as in the UK, that role has been performed by a central bureaucracy, not surprisingly in a bureaucratic manner. While well-meaning, the UK Home Access model (Tolley, 2010), recently terminated by the new Coalition government, was a classic bureaucratic arrangement detached from the everyday realities of life.

Option 2b

There is little to be lost in the school providing the advice; indeed, there is much goodwill and ease of operation to be gained.

Option 3

The suggestion here is to move from the current duplication of technology, where both the home and the school provide basically the same technology, to a model of complementarity, collaboration and minimisation of waste that allows each party to work with its strengths.

Option 4

This allows the home to decide if it wants to use 24/7/365 network access with the students' technology or to opt for wi-fi enabled gear that is less expensive and operates on the school's secure wi-fi network.

While Option 4b (which some schools are using) will provide some small recurrent savings, be conscious it also sends a strong message that 'we don't really want your gear', thus reducing the opportunity to realise many of the kinds of opportunities identified in Chapter 3. Ask if the spending of a little money could in time save the school appreciably greater recurrent expenditure.

Option 5

This is a key set of options. Here is where the school or the education authority expresses its educational philosophy, its trust in the students and, importantly, its attitude towards collaboration with the home.

When you search BYOT online you will find a plethora of school and education authority BYOT usage policies, and some schools/authorities with none. You will also find they sit along a high collaboration/high student trust to no collaboration/distrust continuum, generally fitting with the observation we made earlier about the two general types of BYOT approach. You will find that across the world many schools and education authorities communicate strong distrust of young people and employ highly bureaucratic access procedures that invariably mandate in fine detail where, when and under what conditions use of the student technology will be allowed. But you'll also find, like in many of the case study schools, procedures that have emerged out of close collaboration with the students and parents that do address the laws of the land and recognise the need to work within agreed parameters, but also approach the daily workings from a position of trust in the students.

Interestingly, a number of that group have also built into the agreement an agreed review period. Significantly, several of the Forsyth

County schools have chosen not to put anything on paper, at least in the early years, to trust the students and to let BYOT grow of its own volition. The comments suggest the trust shown is already bearing immense dividends. In shifting from an utter 'no use of personal technology' policy to one of active encouragement, it might be astute to use a graduated set of steps.

In shaping your policy, even in collaboration with the users, it is vital to emphasise the legal obligations the school has to respect. That said, it is interesting to note the number of mandated policies that openly state the school can take or confiscate a student's personal property. It might be wise to check the legality of that kind of action and the wisdom of committing that policy to print in your particular jurisdiction.

Our legal advice (which we address more fully in Chapter 8) suggests that in most jurisdictions across the developed world it is illegal to take another's property and that the school could be opening itself to possible litigation. Ask yourself how you would react if the principal took away your personal technology; that should give you a fair idea of how a parent might react if the school confiscated their gear, for the same law applies to them.

Your choice here could well decide the effectiveness of your BYOT package, and indeed to what kind of litigation you leave yourself open. It is appreciated you can ask the parents and students to waiver their legal rights, but how then will that additional impediment impact on uptake?

Option 6b

The observation made in relation to option 4b applies equally here.

Option 8b

Those who are used to the school supporting (some might say pandering to) students' every call for help might be appalled at the suggestion that the school no longer provide technology support. The big difference is that one is now dealing with student-owned technology that is cared for and maintained by the students everywhere but in the classroom. The suggestion is that the care be extended. It does place the responsibility for the operation of the technology on the student and home and removes an often considerable financial and logistical burden off the school's shoulders.

This is the approach taken by all the case studies.

CONCLUSION

By now you will appreciate that the choice of the BYOT options is not to be taken lightly or rushed, and that each element of the package can have a profound impact upon success or failure. Similarly, it is hoped that you will also appreciate the fundamental importance of trust in the students and authentic collaboration. Finally, there is the necessity to ensure that the package you opt for fits seamlessly with all the school's wider operations and supports the school's quest to realise its shaping educational vision.

....

MANOR LAKES P–12 COLLEGE

Situation

- Manor Lakes is a newly developed state P–12 college within a new growth area in the western suburbs of Melbourne, Australia.
- The school is part of the Victorian education system and, in marked contrast to the earlier-mentioned Broulee Public School case study, does have considerable autonomy in its selection of staff and the allocation of its resources.
- Although Manor Lakes only opened its doors in 2009, at the time of analysis the school already had 1500 of its planned 2500 student intake.
- As with any major green-field development in its embryonic years, it is a dynamic ever-evolving organisation. Significantly, a sizeable proportion of the staff is young and desirous of using the technology.
- Socioeconomically, the student mix is well below the Australian norm.

Fuller details on the College can be found at:
http://www.manorlakesp12.vic.edu.au/.
Contact: Corrie Barclay, e-Learning Coordinator

BYOT developments

Manor Lakes is one of the first schools in Victoria to adopt a model of BYOT, the approach being identified by the e-learning coordinator as the only way it would be able to sustain the high level of technology throughout the school. His vision is strongly supported by the principal.

The confluence of new school resourcing and the federal government's Digital Education Revolution (DER) funding has enabled the school to have wi-fi access across the campus, digital instructional technology in all classrooms and most students having 1:1 computer usage. Fuller details of the school's technology set-up can be found at: http://www.manorlakesp12.vic.edu.au/College-Staff/ ITCMLC.aspx.

Conscious that the school could not sustain the present situation, it set about consulting with the parents of its prospective Year 6 and Year 7 students in the latter part of 2011 regarding the best way forward. The parents chose to go with iPads, with the parents being given the choice of acquiring the desired model of the iPad through the school, over time or through a local provider. It bears reiterating that this is a lower socioeconomic community and yet all the students in the pilot group have acquired their own technology.

That usage began at the start of 2012. Where the school moves next has yet to be decided.

Of note is that the school continues to ban the use of the students' other mobile technology in the school.

CHAPTER **6**

IMPLEMENTATION PRINCIPLES

By now you will have recognised that there is a set of principles that should guide your implementation of BYOT. In this chapter we reiterate those principles that have come to the fore, often unwittingly, in the more successful case studies. While for convenience we have examined each individually, you will soon appreciate their interrelatedness and the imperative of seeking to integrate the set simultaneously into the school's operations.

THE PRINCIPLES

100 per cent student uptake

To take advantage of the kind of opportunities identified in Chapter 3 and achieve the associated outcomes, you will want all your students using their own technology in the school as soon as desired and feasible. At the least, you will want a critical mass of students—in the region of 70–80 per cent—before you can begin realising the major dividends.

The early literature implies all the students will rush to use their gear in the classroom and will do so even when the usage is markedly constrained. But by now you ought to appreciate such thinking is a gross misreading of the aspirations and astuteness of young people and their families. The case study experience already reveals schools are going to have to work hard and smartly over a significant period to achieve the desired 100 per cent student usage and sustain it in the years ahead.

As you examine the variables you must get right, you'll appreciate how challenging it will be for even a capable, digitally aware leadership to reach that figure, let alone sustain that level of usage. Indeed there is the chance that a significant proportion of schools, although adopting BYOT, will never reach total student usage or harness anywhere near all the potential opportunities.

Normalisation

Allied to the 100 per cent goal should be the desire to normalise the usage of BYOT, to make it as natural a part of modern schooling as the pen and paper have been in traditional schooling. The aim from the outset should be for BYOT to become invisible and ubiquitous.

Equity

As mentioned at several points, if at all feasible every one of your students should be provided with the appropriate technology and not left behind. It is appreciated that some might not be of that view, but the research revealing how disadvantaged those without technological tools are educationally, socially and economically prompts us to go out on a limb and put in the bid for each child.

Let BYOT evolve

There appears to be a strong case to factor into your implementation the freedom, time and flexibility to allow BYOT to grow naturally in your school, shaping it only when the need arises. We appreciate this idea might appear alien to many administrators, but the experience of some astute school and education authority leaders in the case studies strongly points to the desirability of ceding some of the control, not over-planning and allowing time for the development to grow and take its own form.

Significantly, the leaders of Forsyth County and the leadership of St Mary, Broulee, Coal Mountain and South Forsyth High have all identified the need to allow BYOT to evolve naturally and—as Frank Pitt, the principal of St Mary Star of the Sea, indicated—to give it an occasional nudge. Strikingly, several of the Forsyth County schools have even chosen not to document the BYOT usage arrangements but simply to trust the students.

Attraction

Recognise in every move you make that you are going to have to attract the students' usage and the ongoing endorsement of their parents, and in many cases grandparents and carers. It requires the school and its leadership to be proactive, strongly articulating the benefits of BYOT to the school, each student and their parents and constantly encouraging the use of the technology in the classroom. There is nothing to be gained and much to be lost by the leadership being apathetic.

For most schools, be conscious of the fact that you will be doing an about-face, having banned (and rationalised that ban) the student technology for years while you are now asking them for their support. They might rightly be sceptical and question the authenticity of your overtures. It will take time and the school's strong proclamation in word and deed to attract their support. Any hints by the leadership or a teacher that the students' technology is not wanted, any unnecessary impediments to student use or any infrastructure shortcomings are likely to be viewed negatively by the students.

Incentives

It is interesting to note the number of case studies that have chosen to combine the attraction with a degree of push by offering incentives. They need only be small. Schools could:
- offer parent workshops on the new technology
- have the students demonstrate the educational use of the technology
- use iPads as prizes in school competitions
- recognise students in publications for the work done with their own gear
- encourage vendors to demonstrate the latest technology to both the students and parents.

All these moves reinforce to both the students and their parents the educational value that the school attaches to the mobile technology.

Provide the purpose

One of the most powerful incentives is providing clear and strong purposes for the students to use their technology at school, both in the classroom and in everyday communication, administration and organisation. Of note is that the case study schools have—perhaps unwittingly—used the strategy as soon as the first of the students began bringing their mobile technology to school. While the in-class use is the most powerful motivator, encouraging students to use a digital organiser instead of a paper diary, communicating individually with the students over their devices and employing school apps also help to send the message to all students that the school wants to make astute use of their gear.

Trust and respect

The students, in particular, but to a degree also the parents, will be strongly influenced by the trust and respect shown to them by the school. Thus far and often unknowingly schools have daily demonstrated their distrust of the students and failed to recognise the 24/7/365 use and care of the students' own technology. Their out-of-school self- or peer-teaching and learning is often dismissed as mere play and accorded no recognition in any school or education authority or certificate.

While virtually every young person has prime operational responsibility for the care and maintenance of their own suite of digital technology, for nearly 80 per cent of the year there are few classroom situations where they can use the digital without the supervision of a teacher. Cyber walls around the school and strict usage parameters proclaim to students that the teachers and authorities do not trust them.

The contrasting scene in those case study schools that have communicated their trust in the students is dramatic. Talk with the leadership of Forsyth Central High and South Forsyth High and they will speak of the immense dividends already flowing from the trust they have accorded the students, the pleasing impact it has had upon student–teacher relationships and the readiness of the students to use their technology sensibly in class. Rather than the angst generated when trying to futilely ban the technology, the focus is now on its astute use.

Operational responsibility

One of the more effective ways of demonstrating your trust is to hand over to each student full operational responsibility for the choice, care and maintenance of their own suite of mobile technology used for school. Remove the school support and pampering. Let them, like all of us, make mistakes and learn from the experience; let them (like the dummies among us) put their iPhone in their back pocket and sit on it! Let them forget their log-in and have to acquire a replacement.

By all means, be supportive of any theft within the school and harsh on any perpetrators, but in general terms move as swiftly as you can to use the same arrangements that the students employ outside the school walls. The research (Green & Hannon, 2007) makes it clear that in the world outside school young people turn in the main to their peers and increasingly the expertise available via Google or YouTube for support— but most assuredly not usually to their teachers. So, let them do in the school grounds what occurs in the outside world.

Collaboration

Another strong statement of trust is authentic collaboration. As is hopefully now clear, collaboration between the students, the home and the school is central to 100 per cent student uptake and the sustained and successful realisation of the myriad dividends possible with BYOT. If you force BYOT upon the parents and students, experience, commonsense and the case studies show not only will the school not achieve anything near 100 per cent student uptake, the students will express in class their ongoing antipathy, with many seeking to undermine the control over the model.

BYOT should be an expression of the authentic collaboration between the home and the school. As flagged earlier, it is a natural flow-on from successful collaborative teaching that sees the home teaching their young people in collaboration with the school.

The school therefore needs to respect and actively recognise the contribution the home has made to the teaching of young people from birth. A key test of that respect, which will be closely watched by both your students and their parents, will come in the choice of the student technology usage procedures. Are you prepared to forgo the need to document the BYOT operational arrangements? Alternatively, are you willing to collaborate with all your students in identifying those arrangements, listen to and respect the expertise of those students and adopt their negotiated arrangements even when you perceive some shortcomings? Is the principal prepared to run with the perceived 'less than perfect' model and willing to be proven wrong or to fine-tune the arrangements at an agreed review date? Or will they only accept the views of their 'ICT experts' and so communicate to the students the school's distrust of their thinking?

It is interesting to note in the case studies how astute the students have been in identifying appropriate arrangements, how ready they are to review those arrangements at a time in the future and how accepting they are of the arrangements decided upon.

Communication

Any who have been associated with major organisational change like this will appreciate the importance of constantly communicating the key facets of the change—and even then some will still complain that they weren't told!

In your implementation strategy, factor in from the outset an astute, apposite, highly efficient and largely digital BYOT communications operation that keeps the school community briefed on the rationale and the developments, and assists the school in addressing the other implementation principles. The imperative of the quality digital communications suite mentioned earlier will become increasingly obvious.

Synergy

BYOT assists the school in becoming predominantly digitally based in its operations and achieving efficiencies and levels of synergy not possible in paper-based organisations. Digital convergence opens the way for the one operation to be used for multiple purposes and the realisation of multiple outcomes when seamlessly integrated with the existing operations.

The students' all-pervasive use of the digital in and out of the classroom can make a significant contribution to the quest for greater synergy. When all within the school's community—the teachers, parents and students— have normalised the use of the digital and have the digital all the time, your school should be asking hard questions about whether paper should be used in any aspect of the school's administration and communication.

Think networked

Allied to the quest to run an ever-more efficient and productive operation and for the ready availability of the digital is the importance, as mentioned earlier, of planning within a networked operational paradigm, with a mindset attuned to getting the most from the opportunities opened up by the networked technology. It is not easy at this point in the evolution of schooling. The natural inclination is to default to the old ways of doing things, to think one has to make do with what is in the school and not consider that the openings that the technology and collaboration have provided.

Personalise 24/7/365 teaching and learning

At the moment your school, like most across the developed world, is likely concerned only with what happens within the school walls, behind (usually closed) classroom doors, where the professional teacher has responsibility for teaching a sizeable group of students a common curriculum, geared in general terms to the norm of the class.

Over the last 50 years, various endeavours have been made to better personalise that teaching, but a significant impediment has been the lack of effective personal technology to support the teacher's efforts. One of the authors can well remember his efforts in the 1960s to individualise the enquiry-based teaching of modern history with 36 students, with only the support of an Imperial typewriter, a Gestetner ink duplicator and an 8 mm strip projector.

BYOT, where the students have ready access to their own suite of digital technology, opens the way for all teaching to be appreciably more personalised. It is an opening that should be used to advantage.

Significantly, the BYOT suite of personal technologies (as flagged in Chapter 3) also provides the school and classroom teachers with a direct connection to the students' out-of-school mode of teaching and learning and the chance to take on board the apposite facets of that model. It is a development both the primary/elementary and secondary case study schools are already seeking to use. BYOT thus not only provides the opportunity to more fully personalise the teaching in the classroom, but also to support a more collaborative mode of teaching.

Student-centred teaching

The greater personalisation of teaching that makes astute use of the students' own suite of digital technologies carries with it a school-wide need to shift to a strongly student-centred style of teaching or pedagogy. It is a vital move your school ought to proclaim when announcing its move to a BYOT model.

Not only does the move fit the desired educational agenda, it also has major implications for the school's realisation of the 100 per cent uptake. It is already clear from the case study schools that the students won't take their technology to those classes where it is not used, and these are invariably the classes that are highly teacher-centred where the teacher provides little or no opportunity for the students to tap into the power of the technology.

Cognitive readiness

In Chapter 1, mention was made of the body of research—long apparent since the developmental studies of Piaget—of the general inability of children to think critically until about the age of 10. The strong suggestion is that until then (around Year 4), the young person's use of the Web needs to be supervised in the home, on the move and in the school.

Clearly this has implications for any primary school's BYOT approach. It is, however, appreciated that there are wi-fi based technologies like the iPod touches that could be used appropriately by younger children under supervision, but all we want to flag is the principle of addressing cognitive readiness in your planning. Interestingly, in the Broulee Public School case study, the students have opted without any school advice to primarily bring iPod touches to school. That said, Broulee has long been an Apple school. On the other hand, Coal Mountain Elementary School, which had been a Windows school, has had the students bring all manner of personal devices.

Integration

As schooling goes digital and networked and normalises the use of the digital, the school will take advantage of the convergence facility of the digital and increasingly integrate all its operations.

The onus on the school leadership to tightly integrate all the school's operations inside and outside the school walls, enhance efficiencies and remove waste is intensifying. The seamless integration of BYOT into all your school's operations should be to the fore in your planning. It should, as mentioned, be integrated into all facets of the school's administration, student organisation, communications and accounts.

While BYOT is a concept that might be initiated by an individual, a faculty or a committee, you should move swiftly to ensure those efforts are soon drawn into the school's wider development. BYOT should never become a 'bolt-on' operation run by a subgroup sitting outside all other school operations.

KISS

The old adage of 'keep it simple, stupid' is one to bear in mind as you embark on the BYOT implementation and everyday management arrangements. When one considers the other core principles that have to be embodied in those operational arrangements—like attraction, purpose, trust, collaboration and student-centred teaching—it should come as no surprise to note the simplicity of the arrangements used in the more astute case studies.

Support and training

As with any other significant change, one needs to build appropriate support, advice and training for all the key parties—teachers, students and parents—into the implementation and transitioning process. By now it should be obvious that one is talking training and support appropriate for a particular school and community. Gone is the 'one size fits all' external package.

With the case studies, it is interesting to note both the variety of ways employed to provide the support and training, online and face-to-face, and how easy the teachers and students have found the move. It is appreciated these are schools that have gone digital and in essence have already 'done the training'.

There is one key area where support could well be needed and that is the secure storage of the student technology when it is not in use. It is appreciated many schools already have both secure personal lockers and battery recharge facilities, but it is an issue that could impact on BYOT uptake in your school.

Respect personal ownership

In shaping the implementation strategy and operational arrangements, a significant new variable to be kept in mind that could also impact on the 100 per cent student uptake is the due regard to the students' ownership of their personal suite of technologies and the contents therein. The students' or parents' ownership of the technology fundamentally changes the situation the school and teachers have thus known.

That change of circumstances needs to be understood together with the implications for the teaching. One needs to consider here both the ethical or moral and the legal aspects. In most developed nations today, both aspects are covered by the laws of the land that prevent others—including teachers—from taking that technology without consent and accessing the information on that technology. In brief, in most developed nations the school and its staff are not entitled to access the information stored on another's personal technology. The student can offer it up but in most situations cannot be compelled to do so. Common sense and years of teaching experience suggest it would be daft for a teacher or even an education authority to try to do so.

It bears remembering the students will be using in class a suite of multipurpose technologies that they are already using 24/7/365 for all manner of purposes, and that will naturally carry all their personal communication. A teacher would be horrified if a principal demanded to see the information on their personal smartphone or took that phone and scrutinised what was there. The principal would be liable to prosecution. The same privacy laws apply to the students' technology.

Primacy of BYOT

The School A case study highlights what one would have assumed was obvious: as soon as the principal decides the school is moving to adopt a model of BYOT, they need to make it clear that the school will begin the transition from a situation where it provides all the personal technology to one where the students will provide the technology. In the School A case, the principal did not provide that clarity but rather prompted two competing models to clamour for primacy at the expense of the students.

Measure uptake

From the outset, the school should put in place simple, easy-to-analyse arrangements for measuring the pace and nature of the student BYOT uptake. This data will be vital to the ongoing evaluation and refinement of your implementation strategy and the movement towards 100 per cent uptake. Make it simple for teachers—or if you prefer, the students—to log their initial use of BYOT on the wi-fi network or database.

CHECKLIST

Table 6.1 *Implementation principles—a summary*

100% student uptake
Normalisation
Equity
Let BYOT evolve
Attraction
Incentives
Provide the purpose
Trust and respect
Operational responsibility
Collaboration
Communication
Synergy
Think networked
Personalise 24/7/365 teaching and learning
Student-centred teaching
Cognitive readiness
Integration
KISS
Support and training
Respect personal ownership
Primacy of BYOT
Measure uptake

CONCLUSION

In reflecting on the applicability of these principles for your situation, it is hoped you'll appreciate the challenge of securing and sustaining 100 per cent BYOT usage, the unlikelihood of any 'top-down' implementation strategy gaining any real traction and the necessity of genuinely trusting, collaborating with and respecting the contribution all will make to the school's BYOT implementation strategy.

NOADSWOOD SCHOOL

Situation

- Noadswood School is an academy and sports college of approximately 1100 Year 7–12 students, situated in the older part of Southampton, UK.
- As a government-funded academy the school has greater freedom than most other UK schools to shape its own educational vision and program, select its staff and allocate its resources.
- Since the mid-2000s, the school has striven to provide a more personalised education and to work more collaboratively with its parents in the holistic teaching of its students. It has been recognised for the part it has played in the Learning Futures Project.
- Socioeconomically, the student group sits above the UK norm.

Fuller details on the school and its program can be found at:
http://www.noadswood.hants.sch.uk/.
Contact: Dr Tim Ennion, Deputy Principal

BYOT developments

It should be stressed that Noadswood has not yet formally adopted a model of BYOT. Rather, the school is one that Lee and Ward examined as part of their work on collaborative teaching (Lee & Ward, forthcoming).

However, what is increasingly evident at the school is that close collaboration with the students' homes and the normalised use of the digital by the teaching staff have already moved the school into the early phase of a BYOT approach.

Vitally, the school is well resourced with the required technology in every teaching room, wi-fi access across the campus and a student group where each of the students has their own suite of digital technologies. Informally, students' use of their own technology is growing.

As the Noadswood leadership looks to the next phase of personal technology resourcing, like many other schools in a comparable situation it will be obliged to give careful consideration to a mode of BYOT.

CHAPTER 7

TECHNICAL HINTS

Your major challenge in the astute introduction of BYOT will be a human one. There are, however, some key technical aspects you need to understand and address in your implementation.

As you come to better understand those issues you will also recognise that for many schools the introduction of BYOT will oblige the school in a relatively short period to fundamentally change the model of technological support it provides, to shift from a 'one size fits all' control-over model to one that facilitates and supports the students' use of their technology.

There could be implications. This chapter examines the technical requirements to be considered if you are to achieve the desired level of student usage. It is written with the school or district executive in mind, with the aim of informing dialogue with those who manage the technology. Hence it is relatively jargon free, but assisted by a brief addendum where some of the more important but little understood concepts are explained.

THE TECHNOLOGY

Aren't we talking about bringing your own devices?

Concentration on the device rather than the technology can mislead and distract. The word 'device' is a big category, and most people interpret this to be a smartphone or a pad/slate of some sort.

Believe it: size doesn't matter. Cameras, MP3 players, indeed the memory card in your camera need to be considered as well as the traditional netbooks, laptops and desktops. The important thing is that they can all allow ubiquitous access to your stuff.

Ubiquity means anywhere, any time, but also implies specificity. Hence our smartphones can do many of the things that a laptop or desktop can, but may not have the right form factor (keyboard size, screen size, processor power). This form factor qualification also includes storage. Online ('cloud') storage has changed all that. iCloud, SkyDrive, Box.net, DropBox and Bitcasa are only some of the online storage facilities available when your internet connection is live.

Some feature a local 'cache' of data for offline use, re-synching the local and online storage when reconnected. This re-synching is vitally important if a variety of devices is to be used. Finish with one and pick up on another: the document you are working on or reading on your laptop is automatically on your iPhone when you get on the train. Also bear in mind that a relatively small expenditure can purchase a 64GB SD card or USB drive, and the operating system on some laptops and desktops allows booting from these storage facilities, providing the full environment of the user on the machine.

The most important thing to keep in mind is that if a device is personal, then the owners need to take responsibility for it. Additionally, the personal nature of the device means that no-one can be guaranteed to be using the same application, file format or even approach to research, knowledge creation or dissemination. This basic shift in ownership implies changes in not only the type of technology deployed, but also in technology and its deployment, policy, personnel and pedagogy.

If we look at learning specifically, older devices will not have the processing power of the newer. The school will need to be careful that teachers don't end up accepting the 'lowest common denominator' of usage, with everyone limited to web browsing and email. Learners' 'market forces' will work against this, however—but this may cause friction, or at least 'device envy'.

For the moment, we will focus on the technology.

Wi-fi or 'wireless' issues

Wireless is a given in the BYOT environment. It acts as the glue to connect devices to each other and to the wider internet, and is increasingly expected to be available across the campus and not simply in the 'teaching rooms'. In this section, we discuss wireless Local Area Networking (LAN) as distinct from 3G or 4G wireless connectivity that mobile phone carriers supply. The school can provide wi-fi LANs but has little control over carrier networks like Telstra, Vodafone, Verizon or BT.

Density and coverage

The difference between density and coverage is important in the provision of adequate wi-fi for members of your community. Many people concurrently using the network (such as in a library space) will require considerable density; a building with fewer users may need to focus on coverage. The two are not mutually exclusive, but require a slightly different set-up.

Vendors often refer to the need for a site survey and the generation of a 'heat map' that will overlay a plan of the buildings with wireless coverage, so that the proper balance between density and coverage can be made. However, like trying to determine the location of concrete pathways for a new school on a green-field site, the location of wireless access points may need to be determined organically rather than solely by computer simulation. Use the heat-mapping exercise as a guide, then work out from your own knowledge of your school where you think the access points should be.

It would be wise to spend some quality time with a systems integrator rather than a wireless vendor so that switchgear, core switching, servers and gateways all work together. An integrator can be charged with making it all work, rather than the 'he said, she said' arguments when network elements from different vendors are interconnected.

An online comment space will allow students and teachers to report high and low performance, and you can fill in the gaps as needed. Point your community at a tool such as speedtest.net, which will give an objective view of network performance. Show them how to capture a screenshot and email it to the responsible person, or perhaps put it up on a community shared space so that the good news can be reported alongside the areas that may need fixing.

Users will expect a quick response and this will require some spare access points and cabling outlets. A general rule of thumb is that additional cabling outlets should be deployed whenever any network expansion is carried out to allow for such organic growth in the future;

it's not only cheaper this way, but provides a much more agile response to changes in need.

Calculations regarding bandwidth

Bandwidth basically means how much data can flow through a communications channel in a given time period. 'How much bandwidth do I need?' is a frequently asked question and tricky to answer accurately, but here's a good general outline.

At home, users would expect to share an Asymmetric Digital Subscriber Line (ADSL) 2+ service, which means around 10 megabits per second (Mbps) download, and 500 kilobits per second (Kbps) in upload, for the average of four people in the house. To provide an equivilent level of service, for every 100 users at the school, you would need to provide the equivalent of 25 ADSL lines, or 250 Mbps. Quite a large amount. Additionally, students will want to upload data as well, so the asymmetric bandwidth of 10 Mbps down and 500 Kbps up for each ADSL equivalent won't hold—you will need a symmetric pipe to the internet.

Of course, you could allow for a smaller bandwidth, but if students can get the higher capacity on their phones, they will bypass the school's network and use their carrier's network instead—with no school filtering or monitoring possible. There is one rule when it comes to bandwidth: you can't have too much of it. The designers of national networks such as Australia's National Broadband Network (NBN) are to be praised for their long-sighted view of future needs.

Your systems integrator should be able to organise your switch/ gateway appliances to shape network traffic so that high-priority traffic always gets through and time-wasting traffic carries a lower priority. But be careful that this doesn't end up with no-one wanting to use your network because it is too restrictive.

For example, some in your school may question the usefulness of YouTube and ascribe it a lower priority in traffic shaping. Yet surveys will show that an increasing number of students use YouTube as their primary search engine. Watching and copying are more important to students than reading and trying to emulate. comScore (2011) reports YouTube searches make up in excess of 30 per cent of all Google searches.

The most significant issues here are that desire for increased bandwidth will only increase and that different people will use different resources. Opportunities for feedback are essential. This is ultimately a people problem, not a technological problem.

IMPLICATIONS

Network issues

Isolation

Sensitive and mission-critical data that the school uses in its administration and record keeping really need to be separated from the student network. Viruses and other malware are the first issue that may come to mind, but also consider the speed impact of student use on administrative function. If networks are shared, conflicts will arise—the networks need to be separated.

There are several ways to do this. Most common is a Virtual Local Area Network (VLAN), but if this network is broadcast on the same wireless access points you will still get crowding, as the wireless network is a shared device. Separate wireless access points with staff-specific security may be required.

Proxy issues

A BYOT program should ideally be platform agnostic, but some devices won't work with proxies (see TechTalk) or require additional software and configuration to do so. This is often outside the expertise of the general public or simply not available on the device in question.

In addition, you may need to revisit your policies regarding filtering of websites. In many schools, some cloud storage areas are blocked and will prevent the sharing of work.

Printing

Hopefully, most of the traditional printing needs in your school will have evaporated after a full implementation of BYOT. However, in a lead-up or transitional period there may be a need to commit to paper. Printing can be quite awkward in this scenario. Traditionally, conversations with the IT department when multi-platform access to printers is mooted results in lots of head shaking and murmurs about print control and print drivers.

Most newer printers on the market have anticipated the multi-device approach and will print documents emailed to them or will provide a web interface for uploading of the file to be printed.

Applications

'Apps' is the new name for programs and they can be installed from a variety of locations, some which are device-specific. For example, the Apple App Store will provide apps that only work on its ecosystem of devices. Likewise, the Android store only works with Android phones and pads/slates, and the Microsoft store works with its Windows Mobile devices.

This may appear to present a roadblock, but only if specific apps are required, and perhaps you will need to think more widely than that. Each platform provides word processors, web browsers, email clients, social networking apps and so forth. In most cases there is little difference between them in terms of what they can achieve. There are differences in how they achieve it, and this may scare some teachers who are used to a more homogeneous technical landscape.

The funding of such apps now moves from a site-licensed model and takes on the same profile as a stationery list. A list of functionalities, rather than specific apps, needs to be communicated to students and parents. In the same way as you don't specify a particular brand or style of ballpoint pen, you may not need to specify a particular app.

One of the benefits of this approach is that students and teachers will move away from the 'open Microsoft Word and …' approach. Additionally, students and teachers will find themselves sharing apps that they have found useful in their learning. Note the traditional teacher approach of 'providing resources' to their students is turned on its head.

Some technologies will not allow certain types of application. For example, Apple's iPad, iPhone and iPod will not allow programming languages such as Scratch or Logo to run. Similarly, these devices will not show Flash-enabled sites (but this is becoming less of an issue as the world moves to a more modern way of displaying video and animation). Specific-purpose apps may need to be used on other equipment (see 'Use someone else's' on p. 90).

Power

While battery technology has improved greatly over the years, batteries may still not be up to a full day's use if the program is successful. Moreover, asking students to 'bring a spare battery' won't work for those devices that have non-removable batteries.

General Purpose Outlets (GPOs) for plugging in chargers need to be in accessible and safe places. It takes a while to charge even a phone and the user may not be able to 'hang around' for that time. In addition, GPOs may be fitted to skirting boards and a charger may not be able to be plugged in as it cannot clear the floor.

Recommended technologies

For the above reasons, a list of recommended devices together with its corollary list of devices not recommended may be a worthwhile program for a school to develop. This list need not be a 'yes' or 'no' list, but will need careful explanation as to why certain devices are not recommended. (Avoid using inflammatory terms such as 'blacklist').

The school could adopt a policy of preventing students connecting to non-recommended devices; however, the managerial overhead here is great. Referring users' to the published list when things don't work may be a better alternative. Inevitably, be prepared for a lot of 'I wasn't aware of that' when a student's new 'Epsilon 4000' handheld device given to them for their birthday won't work on your network. Consultation and constant communication is the only remedy for this.

If you are to build a 'recommended' and 'not recommended' list, ensure it is updated regularly. The authors know of schools that banned the use of phones with cameras because they did not want inappropriate images floating through the internet. Now what phone doesn't have a camera? And with the small sizes of lenses, who could tell anyway?

Support

Parents' assumptions

Parents may assume the school will prevent problems, fix issues or take responsibility for loss or damage. Again, careful communication outlining the school's position is paramount.

Your technology team may assist in connecting a device to the school network (or perhaps use the suggested device list to point out why not). However, they will need careful training to recognise the shift from the repair mentality needed for a school-supplied technology program and the newer situation where the student takes responsibility for their device.

The school needs to decide whether it applies this approach with all groups. It can delegate total responsibility (even to the very young), work with a mix of school- and parent-supplied technology for the younger students, or hold off moving into that area until the teachers feel ready. Of note is that Broulee has handed responsibility to the Year 4–6 students, while Coal Mountain has opted to do it—albeit with sensitive teacher observation—for all the elementary school years.

In the land of paper, privacy issues relate to who has taken or copied whose material, but the interconnectedness of modern technologies means that a student's work or image or other sensitive data is only a click away from going viral on a social network. The fact that students will have their photographs taken by others and then put into a public space will challenge us all. It will happen, often with the best of intentions, but will be ameliorated by outlining and teaching the responsibilities that we all now face with our connected technologies.

Bring your own

Variety

'Technology' includes more than just a computer. iPhones, MP3 players, slates, netbooks, laptops or even gaming machines fit this description. Indeed, a USB stick can contain a student's total environment with connectivity to cloud-based storage and applications.

In promoting or discussing the program, stress the need for 'recent' modern technologies or otherwise specify a technology that is not handed down. We must accept that any particular technology is evanescent, losing its power through a range of age-related issues such as diminished battery life, incompatibility with newer wireless access points or applications, or just being too slow to keep up with an enquiring and creative mind.

If the program is successful, students will be doing far more than the four-year-old laptop from mum's work can handle. This needs to be stressed and parents guided past the 'I only bought it five years ago' view.

Use your own

Responsibility is the keyword here. Not only will users need to take responsibility for charging, maintaining and bringing their technology to school (and to class), but also for matters such as Bluetooth privacy and personal hotspots.

Firstly, Bluetooth (short range radio networking protocol designed for personal use, say between a laptop and a phone) can expose a user's device to snooping by others if the process is not well understood. Sending a photo from one student to another is a good use for Bluetooth networking, but giving a fellow student access to another's phone, pad or laptop could end in tears if data is (intentionally or not) erased or compromised.

The fellow student may not be the perpetrator of this: another individual on the bus home may scan for and compromise data on a student's phone if it is left in a mode suitable to have its radio broadcasts captured and analysed. As phones move more and more to 'digital wallets', this will become a big issue if not well understood.

Secondly, most phones can now take a carrier's signal such as a 3G or 4G data service and re-broadcast it on wi-fi. Referred to variously as 'personal hotspots' or similar, sharing one user's 3G data access with others is convenient, but it will cause reliability issues if more than three personal hotspots are set up in the same area (see 'TechTalk: Wi-fi specifications').

Use someone else's

In some cases, your own technology might not be up to par. Like the sports car owner who needs to go camping, you may need to leave the convertible in the garage and borrow a 4WD because it is the right vehicle for that particular job. Hence, especially in the short term, schools may find themselves in the seemingly retro position of providing computer labs or perhaps cubicles with machines specifically set up for projects involving CAD/CAM, High End Video, or programming and other computer science projects, which may not be accessible to the devices that students bring to school.

Furthermore, someone may also have a better camera/GPS/ robotics app/doodad that you need. The borrowing of another student's equipment already happens, but not always with a several-hundred-dollar device, and not necessarily with implied access to the owner's life. Again, care with the development and promulgation of a responsible use policy is required.

Finding your own stuff

The responsibility for where data is stored ultimately rests with the users—teachers will get tired of 'the internet ate my homework'. For many, this is a challenge, even when their data is stored on a local drive, so schools would be advised to instigate specific storage sites that will be recommended to users and provide clear instructions for access.

Staff and administrative data will need separate storage locations. Whether these are at the school or in the cloud is up to the school, but attention will need to be given to the continued and uninterrupted access to those data needed to run the school.

Students who are attempting major works that are stored digitally will need additional advice regarding the reliability of storage devices. Schools would be wise to consider a disclaimer regarding their responsibility for student-stored data or to provide local secure networked storage specifically for this purpose.

Sharing your stuff—collaboration

The fact that user-supplied devices may not have a common file format means the school may need to provide an online facility, such as Google Docs, as a school standard. If a piece of work is to be assessed, it needs to be accessible. Students and teachers will need to be made aware of this in terms of format and access. (Personal or copyright reasons may make it inappropriate, for example, to have a work publically accessible.)

What do existing IT personnel do now?

Moving to a BYOT scheme means no more need to image machines, fix application issues and warehouse loaner machines or organise repairs, and manage inventory and licensing. These entail a lot of person hours so you will need to figure out what to do with existing personnel. Of course, there will always be administration, servers, (shudder) printers and wireless access points to be managed, but this could be outsourced. It will be well worthwhile asking 'What skills do my IT team have now?' as part of BYOT planning. Many will be suited to training and in the development of systems to support such a venture.

Corporate IT

The likes of Microsoft, Adobe and Apple stand to lose millions when their control of who does what with which device is challenged. As such, they will fight to preserve the status quo. Expect drastically reduced site licensing, or applications and functions tied to a specific device. Also expect pressure from the usual suspects: 'The kids need to use what industry is using' and similar war cries.

A simple online search of 'corporate BYOT' will expose how the corporate world is moving to a BYOT model. While the corporate application of BYOT is being challenged by privacy and IP issues (as company data may be located on employees' personal devices), no such challenge exists with student data. There may be challenges with staff equipment, but this is no real change to the existing situation, as staff who are given a laptop that contains student personal data can already copy these to a USB stick or similar. Clear policy and procedures will win over technological solutions here.

'Industry expects conformity' and so forth is similarly a dying argument. Rarely are we now faced with instructions such as 'the manuscript needs to be presented in Times New Roman, 12 point, double-spaced and single-sided', because the device on which the recipient is reading the document may be a laptop or Kindle, an iPad or a smartphone, all with differing and user-customisable formats. Specifications such as style guides will also change, concentrating more on communication, with rules that rely on the user having a good sense of visual literacy.

Pressure may also come to bear on how a given corporation can assist schools in the 'management' of devices. But this is really no different from the school-supplied technology of the past and should be eschewed. If the technologies are personally owned, it will be difficult to make a case for managing those devices.

CONCLUSION

We hope these few technical observations will assist your planning. As you will appreciate, the comments are by necessity general in nature as they relate equally to large multi-campus secondary schools and small regional primary or elementary schools. We are assuming that you will tailor your approach to the technical to suit your situation and budget.

There are, however, several key points that bear stressing in establishing the technical platform on which to build your BYOT model.

- You are about to construct a technological support model that will soon become fundamentally different to that provided thus far. You will invariably be moving from a 'one size fits all' approach, where the school selected, acquired, controlled and maintained the personal technology and where in many situations the ICT team controlled the use of that technology, to where the school will be facilitating the students' use of their own technology.

- There should be (if it hasn't already occurred) a ceding of control from the staff and a lift in the trust and responsibility accorded the students.

- The school will want a technology staff that provides the leadership and the technical advice needed to ensure the most effective use of BYOT. It doesn't need a staff more concerned with maintaining the status quo.

- The new model will have major implications for the nature and extent of the support provided by the technology team and may (as flagged) occasion a rethink about the number of personnel needed on staff.

It is thus vital from the onset of your BYOT thinking that the school leadership understand the potential implications and, if required, discuss them with those whose role might change or go.

TECHTALK

ADSL and SDSL

The word 'asymmetric' in Asymmetric Digital Subscriber Line (ADSL) means that upload and download happen at different speeds. As most use of the internet has been the Web, and most people are browsing, then only a small amount of information needs to go out to the internet (the address that you want to browse) compared with the comparatively huge amount coming back from the internet (the downloaded page with its data-bloated images, advertisements, movies and so forth). As users create more data to share on the internet, so upload speed needs to be increased using a Symmetric Digital Subscriber Line (SDSL).

SDSL will also be needed at the school if it intends to push data out to its community. But using services in the cloud will mean that large, school-based servers pumping data out to parents will not be needed—the main reason will be upload to remote servers.

Proxies

When bandwidth to schools was extremely limited, much use was made of proxies at the gateway. A combination of high-memory computer and software would store recently accessed webpages locally so that future requests for those webpages could be delivered from the proxy, saving precious bandwidth to the external internet connection. These machines further developed authentication, so that users could be blocked or have their usage restricted, and also to monitor any given user's traffic.

Because so many websites are now dynamically built, and built to reflect the interests of the individual, local proxying isn't very effective as a bandwidth maximiser. However, because of their duty of care, schools might still want to track users, so monitoring which machine went where and when will still be required.

Bandwidth

Our bandwidth calculation earlier in this chapter tells us that big numbers are involved if we want to provide each student with adequate access. This requirement will only increase. Cisco System's white paper (2011) claims that:

> Annual global IP traffic will reach the zettabyte threshold (one zettabyte is one thousand million gigabytes) by the end of 2015.

> Global Internet traffic will increase fourfold over the next 5 years, growing at a compound annual growth rate (CAGR) of 32% from 2010 to 2015.

> A growing amount of Internet traffic is originating with non-PC devices. In 2010, only 3% of Internet traffic originated with non-PC devices, but by 2015 the non-PC share of Internet traffic will grow to 15%. PC-originated traffic will grow at a CAGR of 33%.

It also claims that:

Traffic from wireless devices will exceed traffic from wired devices by 2015.

Cisco, 2011

It's going to mean more and more and more bandwidth.

The Cloud

The 'Cloud' is essentially a rebranding. To borrow from Bill Clinton's presidential campaign slogan: 'It's the internet, stupid'. Long considered as a download-only facility, the internet has been through two rebrandings—Web 2.0 was a marketing term used to offset the bursting of the internet bubble in the early part of this century, and Cloud similarly rebrands the internet. Both concentrate on the shift of download-only consumption of data on a machine that has locally installed application software to more user-created data, mediated by online applications and storage.

IP connectivity

Internet Protocol (IP) essentially defines the rules of engagement between devices that connect to the internet. One of the rules is that no two devices have the same numerical address, rather like our phone system.

The founders of the internet designed it to work between researchers and workers in largely higher education and military circles, and their initial pool of addresses (4 294 967 296 for those of you playing at home), referred to as IPv4, is not even enough for one device per human on this planet, let alone when you multiply this by an individual's smartphone, VoIP phone, laptop, iPad and desktop. It pales when we realise that every device in our life—our car (which itself has several computers to run it), our washing machine, our delivery truck's location beacon, hey, even our children's location beacons—all need IP addresses.

In the past, we've 'cheated' by shielding our devices behind gateway technologies that translate our internet addresses to single outside addresses. This allowed us to use the same address inside our organisation as our friend's in another organisation, relying on the gateway to present only our publically viewable outside addresses that are peculiar to each company. The sheer number of devices and their mobility (and a few other technicalities, less relevant to this discussion) meant that a redesign was needed and IPv6 was born.

On a historical note, the IPv4 address space was exhausted in January 2011.

> The number of devices connected to IP networks will be twice as high as the global population in 2015. There will be two networked devices per capita in 2015, up from one networked device per capita in 2010.
>
> Cisco, 2011

Wi-fi specifications and speeds

Wi-fi is the (now) commonly accepted term for wireless local area network access. The Institute of Electrical and Electronics Engineers (IEEE) is the body responsible for the maintenance of standards in wireless networking. The 802 standard deals with networking, and the 802.11 standard specifically refers to wireless networking. The IEEE works with the communications authorities that allocate spectrum in differing countries so that frequencies chosen do not interfere with other devices and wireless devices can reliably communicate with each other. There are four commonly used subsets of 802.11: the b, g, a and n standards (more will come as the technology moves forward). Each of these operates on a different frequency and has differing ranges and throughputs.

The important thing here for school planning is that older devices may not be able to take advantage of the greater speeds. To provide coverage for all students' equipment, some will suggest bringing the wireless campus to a 'lowest common denominator' but this will hamper access to internet-based storage. In addition, older devices will be constrained by legacy protocols that may not be supported by the newer wireless access points and schools may need to resort to providing multiple access points in the same physical area for the differing protocols.

Hence, 'hand me downs' will make life more difficult technically and economically. You will need to educate your whole community.

Additionally, most mobile devices (at the time of writing) use a broadcast frequency of 2.4 GHz, which effectively has only three channels. If more than three wi-fi devices broadcast in a small geographical space (say, the same room), interference will render the network unusable.

SOUTH FORSYTH HIGH SCHOOL

Situation

- South Forsyth High School is a public high school of approximately 1600 Year 7–12 students, in Forsyth County, Georgia, USA.
- As part of the Forsyth County School District the school has considerable say over its staffing and its allocation of resources.
- Like the other Forsyth case study schools, South Forsyth works closely with the County office and has benefited from the leadership and support provided by the County, particularly in the use of instructional technology in teaching and learning.
- Significantly, the school, like the other Forsyth case study schools, has on staff both an instructional technology support teacher plus a media specialist.
- Socioeconomically, the student group sits above the USA norm.

Fuller details on the school and its program can be found at:
http://www.forsyth.k12.ga.us/site/default.aspx?domainid=2002.
Contact: Suzanne Korngold, Assistant Principal

BYOT developments

South Forsyth High School's move to a model of BYOT, like the other Forsyth schools, flowed naturally from the school's normalised use of the digital by all staff, but it was also aided by the leadership and support provided by the local education authority's instructional technology unit.

The school has provided all its teachers with their own laptops for some time. All the teaching rooms are equipped with Promethean interactive whiteboards and in all there is ready access to an array of mainly Windows-based technology.

South Forsyth has had ready access to the internet, use of ANGEL, the County's learning platform, and in recent years wi-fi access across the campus.

The school began moving towards a BYOT model in 2011 and since then has largely let the development grow and evolve.

Significantly, while using a core acceptable use policy (http://www.forsyth. k12.ga.us/site/Default.aspx?PageID=22724), the school allows each teacher the flexibility to vary it so long as it is in consonance with the County's policy.

The trust the school has accorded the students is already reaping significant dividends, not simply in improved student–teacher relations, but also in the students' readiness to bring their preferred method of learning from outside the school into the classroom, and to make far greater use of peer support and teaching. South Forsyth High is, almost unwittingly, dismantling the old school walls and blurring the divide between in-school and out-of-school teaching and learning.

What resonated with South Forsyth's move to BYOT was the astuteness of the school's leadership, its holistic grasp of the plethora of variables to be addressed to ensure the development succeeds, and also its recognition that BYOT had to be seamlessly integrated into the school's and County's operations. The leadership was willing to cede control and felt confident enough to allow the development to continue to evolve and not to overplan.

CHAPTER **8**

IMPLEMENTATION AND MANAGEMENT CHECKLISTS

Throughout the chapters we have referred to the importance of adopting a BYOT implementation strategy appropriate for your school at this point in its evolution. We've identified the readiness variables, the model options and the kind of principles to bear in mind in shaping your school's implementation strategy and transitioning arrangements.

It is up to you and your community to translate those thoughts into a working reality. Then allow BYOT to evolve. Be prepared to cede some control and let the development take much of its own course, while closely monitoring its uptake and usage.

To assist in that monitoring, two checklists are provided below: one in relation to the implementation and a second on the in-school management of the students' technology. There are several general issues relating to those checklists we need to underscore.

READY YOURSELF FOR THE FRUSTRATION

In moving to a fundamentally different operational paradigm, you (like the case studies) will regularly encounter people, bureaucratic arrangements, technical set-ups, structures, power groups and possibly legal impediments that will frustrate you no end—and might even incline you to swear!

The situation is likely to get worse before it gets better, for based on past experience it will be some time before many bureaucrats and legal boffins finally understand the full implications of BYOT; until then they will seek to apply the rules and procedures of a bygone era, little appreciating the new reality.

In brief, they will—as always—want to stop the world. Sadly that is a reality for which you ought to prepare. You can use a threat analysis and anticipate many of those frustrations, but in the end you are going to have to work your way around or over most of them. History shows that in time and with the normalisation of the change, those hassles disappear. But for the early adopters it can be a pain that most will experience.

ADDRESSING EQUITY

Reference has already been made to ensuring all students have the appropriate technology and home internet access. We have strongly urged the individual school to have operational responsibility for looking after each student. And while we still hold with the school having the prime operational responsibility, there is much the local education authority and the national government can do to assist.

The provision of appropriate broadband access is a responsibility best handled at the national level. It is thus pleasing to note the concerted moves being made in the UK, the USA, New Zealand and Australia to provide all citizens, including young people, with high-speed internet access and to remove the current black spots. The national government can also provide financial incentives such as tax relief for families of young people to acquire the requisite technology.

However, there is also much that local education authorities can do to assist. There will be pockets where internet access is still substandard and situations where young people cannot afford the technology. Those shortcomings should be quantified at the local level and solutions elicited in conjunction with the schools.

The local authority knows its context, its socioeconomic mix and the sources it can turn to for support, be it the authority itself, a philanthropic trust, major local companies or indeed service organisations that would be willing to assist those in need. An early proclamation from the authority regarding the importance of equity and what it is doing should go a long way to ameliorating many of the community's concerns about BYOT. The schools can then complement the national and local education authority efforts.

The authors' experience in addressing the matter of equity and technology points to the necessity of each school undertaking its own research on each student's situation. All too often equity is used as an excuse for doing nothing. The naysayer's trump card to any educational development involving technology seems to be to cite equity, to dismiss the national research showing near everyone has access and to say its own community is uniquely disadvantaged—invariably without having actually put in the hard yards to find out.

With all parties working together, each school should be able to look after its own.

GRADUATED OR ALL IN?

Does your school opt to pilot the introduction of BYOT with several classes or does it directly involve all the students? It is a decision only you can make, knowing your school's situation and readiness.

The case study schools have opted for both approaches; even those case studies that have normalised the use of the digital throughout the school have used both. The main factor appears to be the staff's readiness to put a toe into the water or to dive straight in. Both eventually will work. Coal Mountain Elementary in Forsyth County, for example, moved with two classes for a semester and then went to 16 classes the next semester. It is your call.

The advantage of starting with a couple of classes or a year level or two is that it can help allay teachers' fears and help remove any glitches before the whole school moves. If, on the other hand, the total staff feel comfortable and are ready to move as a group, as long as the implementation plan remains flexible, the school can move as one to introduce the development.

LAUNCH OR QUIET INTRODUCTION?

Do you employ a high-profile launch of BYOT on a specified date or do you initially simply say to the students, after due consultation and attention to all the details, that they can begin bringing their own technology to class from now on? Again, it has to be your call.

The degree of acceptance of the concept within your parent community and the local political scene will be two important factors. However, in light of the number of observations made earlier about the need for the school leadership to make the school's intention regarding BYOT clear to all, the authors suggest there is much to be gained from having all within the school's community understand the magnitude and implications flowing from the move. That can be assisted by a high-profile launch.

It is interesting to note that a number of the case study schools that have moved naturally to BYOT have opted to let BYOT settle in before publicising the move in the media.

TRACKED LEARNING 'VERSUS' PERSONALISATION

There are some significant developments underway in using the technology to more closely track, analyse and shape student learning. Advocates of that important work, which currently requires all students in the class to have the same computers, are particularly critical of the move to BYOT, the shift away from all students having common computers and the students being able to use any technology they believe is appropriate.

The reality, as we regularly affirm, is that in time all schools will use some form of BYOT. They will also increasingly use different types on individual apps, some stand-alone and some web-based, as well as various online document creation facilities like Google Docs. They will, in brief, use an ever-evolving suite of digital technologies inside and outside the school walls.

The challenge for those developing the student tracking technology is to work with the technology that will be used, and not to have the technology determine what kind of teaching and learning can be done (as has happened too often in the past). In the post-PC world the Microsoft hegemony is no more.

How the sophisticated tracking of the learning is done we will leave to the developers. However, we would strongly suggest that it is not (as we have implied in the subheading) a case of one or the other but rather how to astutely integrate a mix of learning styles in the 24/7/365 teaching of young people.

SPECIALIST AREAS

Early in the book we stress that our focus is on the suite of digital technologies young people already use every day, all year round in their own teaching and learning, and can also use in virtually all classrooms. We also acknowledge that there are some areas of teaching that require specialist technology.

Take, for example, the school orchestra or concert band. Interestingly, in this area over the years in most schools, as the students became more proficient, both the students and the school (state and independent) have employed a 'bring your own technology' model, where the technology in this case is a musical instrument. Significantly, the underlying principle is exactly that of BYOT. In all his years of involvement in youth music, Mal Lee, one of the authors, never encountered anything other than a desire by the school to collaborate with parents and students in the astute use of that technology, to respect the ownership of that technology and for the students to look after it and be responsible for it, even when left on the bus.

We'd suggest you reflect on the music situation as you ponder what to do with the specialist digital technology. Does the school, like a beginner concert band, provide beginner-level technology and move to a BYO model or at least an option at the higher level? What is the best approach for your school's video production, digital art, computer science or digital photography classes? It may be that the school provides most of the high-end technology, both hardware and software; but if, for example, a student prefers to use her own high-end camera or video editing suite, so be it.

While advocating the general use of BYOT, there will be specialist situations in the school where it may well be best for the school to provide the technology. What we suggest is that, like with music, the school adopt the solution that best fits the current needs in each area of learning. Forget a 'one size fits all model' that obliges the one tool to be used in all specialist areas, and most assuredly don't dismiss using a BYOT model.

THE IMPLEMENTATION

By this stage most of the checkpoints each school should be using will be self-explanatory, but there are several that appear for the first time. A brief elaboration of each is included following the implementation checklist.

Table 8.1 *Implementation checklist*

Champions	• Identified fellow champions/doers? All the case studies have had a key driving figure able to assemble a team of other movers around them. • The whole school takes on board the work of the champions?
General strategy	• Identified key elements? • Highly flexible? • Given chance to evolve naturally? • Fit with school's desired direction? • Effectiveness of school's current shaping educational vision? • Tightly integrated?
Principal	• Ready to lead with BYOT? • (If applicable) Education authority acquiescent? • Principal has ensured the school and staff members are safe from litigation?
BYOT package	• School chosen appropriate BYOT package—or indeed non-package?
BYOT operational arrangements	• Students, teachers and parents consulted? • Operational arrangements agreed upon? • Operational arrangements published online?
Disadvantaged students	• Processes underway to cater for those without home internet access? • For example, have you identified who needs support?
Operational basics	Have all the key basics been addressed? For example: • Student internet publishing permissions secured? Importance of having documented parent permissions for every student to publish photo/name/work to the Web. • Parent/student email/mobile phone/Twitter addresses on database? • Secure storage of student technology arranged? • Student technology recharging facilities provided?
Digital communications suite	• Key components in place? • Integrated with communications/promotions/support/training programs?

Table 8.1 *(continued)*

Commence operation of technology and infrastructure	• Ready campus wi-fi access for students? • Adequate bandwidth provided? • Simple student access? • Student responsibility for technology care and maintenance clarified? • Each teaching room has requisite presentation and creation technology? • Adequate personal technology provided by school for the transition? • Technology support team attuned to new role?
Digital resource management	• Appropriate personnel in place? • Phase-in arrangements ready?
Respect for student ownership	• Staff briefed on nation's/state's ownership and privacy laws as relate to 'confiscating' student technology or accessing without permission private information on a student's technology? • Staff discussed moral/ethical/educational reasons for respecting student ownership?
Start date	• BYOT introduction date set? • Nature of the start determined?
BYOT uptake	• Facility in place to record the first time each student uses their technology in class? • Ready facility to record and instantly analyse BYOT uptake for each student? class? year level? designated subgroups (disabled, indigenous, etc.)?
BYOT promotion	• Holistic promotional strategy prepared? • Suite of promotional materials, rationale and opportunities for client comment readied? • Linked to digital communications suite?
Indicative time line	• Prepared indicative time line from time of introduction of BYOT to total uptake? • Preparedness to extend if increased dividends possible?
BYOT costing	• Costed the likely increase in school resourcing with the introduction of BYOT for each of the next three years? • Modelled school's potential recurrent savings for each of the next three school years, based on the indicative time line, the school's BYOT package, current technology commitments and efficiencies possible in school operations? • Identified, costed and budgeted for what the school community needs to do to achieve quality, sustained 100 per cent BYOT usage, in terms of infrastructure, transition technology, software and apps, training and promotion?

Operational basics

The authors' analysis of the shift to a mode of networked schooling and discussions with interested folk at conferences points to the need to remind one to get the operational basics right and to secure any parent permissions required. One of the most commonly forgotten aspects is securing the parents' permission to publish students' photos, name and work to the Web. For sure, there will be some who for various reasons will say no, but the case study experience suggests that if this is done astutely and in a collaborative manner the vast majority will give their permission. It will take time but you will soon appreciate the dividends that flow.

The same effort is required in the first instance with emails and, if required, student mobile phone numbers and Twitter addresses. Arrange to get them at the outset, using a simple online database that also includes the facility for the user to readily update those details, and the going will be much easier.

Legal and ethical aspects of BYOT

The use of students' personal technology in the school will take most schools into the new and potentially litigious area of student privacy and provide a real chance of teachers breaking—perhaps unwittingly—the law of the land. If unsure of your situation, seek some legal advice.

As indicated, in most developed nations there are strong privacy laws designed to prevent others from looking at one's work without permission. In brief, teachers, and even the hallowed principal, have no power under the privacy laws of most developed nations to demand to see what is on another person's technology, be it a teacher's, a parents' or a student's technology.

Some teachers working in their insular world sometimes imagine the law does not apply to what happens in the school. Lower Merion School District in Pennsylvania had to outlay considerable reparation for its 2010 breach of that state's privacy laws (eSchool News, 2010), even though its offence entailed the use of the district's property albeit in the students' homes.

It is important to warn teachers of potential breaches of privacy laws and to discuss the implications for the teaching process. It might be as well to publish this respect for the student's privacy on the school's website, as part of its BYOT section. Related is the importance of also publishing for all interested parties the current BYOT operational arrangements, if the school has opted for that approach.

The students require respect, in the same way that you would expect your privacy to be respected.

Covering one's backside

Allied to the comments on respect for the laws of the land is the imperative of the principal covering their backside, and indeed that of the school staff, in the introduction of BYOT. Protection from complicated legal and administrative issues becomes ever-more important when your school is one of the pathfinders making the move within an education authority.

There will be those whose power base or standing is lessened by the introduction of BYOT. They may well try to stymie the school's move with backstabbing and thus it is important for the principal to move quickly to forestall those efforts. Those who have never worked in a bureaucracy are likely to be saying how unnecessary it is to have to do this, but it is a global reality with which all school leaders have to contend.

Indicative time line

Upon analysing the school's readiness for BYOT, selecting your model and deciding upon your general implementation strategy, you should prepare an indicative time line as to when the school will achieve 100 per cent student uptake. You will find it will guide so many of your subsequent BYOT implementation actions. And yes, you will constantly need to fine-tune the time line in light of the uptake data, but it is a guide all can use.

Transition period

How long it will take for your school to move from its introduction of BYOT to 100 per cent uptake we cannot tell as yet, as we know of no schools that have completed that journey. Based on the case study experience, we have hypothesised on the possibility of well-prepared schools taking several years. Already the signs are that some of the smaller schools could achieve total uptake earlier. We have also suggested that unless approached astutely, some schools might never achieve the total normalised student usage.

However, what is abundantly clear is that the length of that transition period will vary in each school depending on the myriad factors discussed earlier. Variables like school size, readiness, home–school collaboration, resourcing, quality of the school leadership and the astuteness of the school's implementation plan will all have an impact. In most situations the school leadership will be best placed to identify the length of the transition period for the indicative time line.

Monitoring BYOT uptake

It is vital to have in place from day one a record of each student's initial bringing to class of their own digital technology. The wi-fi log-in could be part of the solution.

While the entry should be simple and quick, you will want the facility to explore uptake by:
- each student
- each teacher
- year level
- designated subgroups
- the school as a percentage of the school population.

You might also want to secure some general idea of the type of technology used—smartphone, tablet, netbook and the like. It is a key record for it tells you how well the school is performing on the indicative time line.

The financials

The indicative time line is also essential for estimating the budgetary impact of BYOT on the school's and, in time, the government's finances. Working with the indicative uptake time line and the school's chosen model of BYOT, you should be able to estimate the likely effect on the school's budget for around three years, identifying the anticipated extra resources that will be added to the 'school's coffers' and the concomitant savings the school will be able to make annually.

In referring to the 'school's coffers', we are talking about those potentially considerable resources the students will add to the school's wealth by using their own gear in class rather than using that paid for by the school. For example, if 250 students opted to use their own iPads in class—each worth, for arguments sake, $500—the school's wealth will increase by $125 000.

We'd suggest estimating the figures for three financial years. Identify initially the additional resources the school will likely have to use in each of the next three years: take the estimated number of students that will be using their own technology by the end of each financial year; multiply by the estimated average value of the students' suite of digital technologies; identify as a percentage of the total student cohort.

In calculating the worth of the student package, be sure to include the approximate cost of:

- the hardware
- the software and apps used with the hardware
- any insurance carried
- students' personal telecommunication plans, recognising some students might only opt for wi-fi access.

In examining those additional resources, be conscious of and actively promote any source(s) of financial support the homes can access. For example, in Australia the federal government provides in the region of $750 tax relief each year for each child to acquire and use their own digital technology.

The aforementioned equation should give the school an idea of:

- the annual value of the homes' contribution to the school's 'budget'
- the amount of personal technology and software it needs to provide in each of the three years.

In calculating the likely savings, be conscious of factoring in all the variables and not simply those associated with the gear itself. In many larger schools the recurrent staffing cost savings could be considerable. Consider the following kinds of items. (While we appreciate all might not apply to your situation, equally there could be some distinct to your situation that you need to add.)

- Personal digital technology the school does not have to acquire that year, including interest on that gear, if applicable
- Insurance on the technology not required
- Software not needing to be bought
- Reduction in the number of software licences
- Reduction in equipment maintenance contracts or support staff
- Depreciation of the superseded school-acquired personal technology

- Any specialist communication system the school or the education authority is paying for that will be superseded by the BYOT software and apps, such as high-end video conferencing
- Social and/or material capital contributed by the parents or community as a consequence of the greater collaboration.

In addition to those more obvious savings, consider also the savings made possible with the move to the normalised use of personal digital technology with all within the school's community, and the savings achieved by moving from a paper base to increased efficiencies and enhanced productivity. For example, consider approximate savings in:

- postage
- paper
- photocopying and photocopy technology
- staff, based on an hourly rate of those staff used in the paper-based administration/communication
- staff time spent preparing paper-based teaching materials
- the reduction in the time spent contacting students, preparing lesson materials, personalising teaching and the like.

As indicated, it will also be important to estimate the additional outlay required for the school to make best long-term use of BYOT. The norm with a major organisational change like this is that one has to spend a little more in the short term to achieve the best long-term savings. These costs could be human and technical, upgrading infrastructure to accommodate the extra network traffic, providing training and promoting the 100 per cent uptake. There are already strong indications from the case studies that there will be a continuing, probably escalating demand for extra bandwidth as well as significantly greater traffic—both of which cost. You should then be better placed to understand the financial implications of the development for the school.

BYOT MANAGEMENT

In the BYOT management checklist in Table 8.2 we have focused primarily on the transition phase. While recognising many of the points will remain pertinent with 100 per cent student uptake, our concern in this work is to assist your school to get to that point.

Table 8.2 *Management checklist*

Management	Simple and efficient to manage?
Student usage	Simple and efficient for students to use?
Monitoring usage	Ease of monitoring and analysing the level and nature of each student's and each student cohort's BYOT use of the school wi-fi network?
Network access	Reliable high-speed wi-fi network capable of readily accommodating ever-increasing student use in place?
Transition personal technology	A technology plan in place, in keeping with the BYOT uptake, to transition out the school's personal technology and software commitments?
BYOT uptake monitoring	Scheduled monthly check and analysis of BYOT uptake, and review of the effectiveness of the arrangements in place to promote that uptake?
Teaching encouraging BYOT usage	Monitoring arrangements in place to assess the level of BYOT uptake with each teacher?
Student feedback	Scheduled bimonthly meetings with sample student groups eliciting their views on BYOT?
Student breaches	Scheduled quarterly analysis of data compiled on student transgressions of agreed BYOT operating conditions, identification of any trends and any issues to be addressed?
Review of costing	Scheduled bimonthly analysis of the costs associated with using BYOT and the savings being or potentially being achieved?

Monitoring student usage

At least in the early years of BYOT, it is probably wise to monitor the students' use of BYOT on the school campus. It is easy to monitor each student's use of the school's secure wi-fi network and to use that information when considering the impact of BYOT. Those case studies where there is close collaboration with the students and the homes paint a very positive scene, with remarkably few student hassles. In contrast, in those case studies where the school has not readied itself for BYOT, not surprisingly there are both strong student dissension and abuse of the system in use.

Monitoring the effectiveness of the BYOT implementation strategy

While one's educator mind goes initially to the management of the students, in reality the far greater task for the school and its leadership will be the successful monitoring and management of the uptake of BYOT and the swift attainment of 100 per cent usage. That is why we have included in the management checklist a suite of suggestions on how to maintain the focus on that goal and having the data on which to base any change in strategy or effort.

Teaching that encourages BYOT usage

As indicated early on, there are strong signs that the students don't take their technology to those teachers' classes where the teaching approach doesn't require the use of the technology. In sporadic situations in a secondary school that might not impact on the overall BYOT uptake, but in a primary/elementary school, if there are a sizeable number of those teaching situations, it could significantly impact on the eventual 100 per cent uptake.

Mostly it will be related to teachers favouring a strong teacher-centred pedagogy that involves little student activity. We appreciate that this could be extremely difficult to redress, particularly in situations where the school itself has little say in the choice of its staff. Part of the answer lies in identifying those classes where the students' technology is little used or not used at all. The contrast with the other staff is likely to be marked. The data provides an excellent platform for a professional discussion with the teacher or teachers concerned about what might best be done to change the situation. The ongoing monitoring of the uptake can also assist. But it can be a difficult situation that needs to be handled adroitly, often by the principal.

CONCLUSION

At this point we hand the task of introducing BYOT in your school over to you and in the next chapter provide some preliminary thoughts on how you might assess the impact of BYOT.

SCHOOL A

Situation

- After analysing this case study and identifying major errors of judgement by the leadership, we believed it was important to describe the situation, to flag the mistakes made, but to not specifically identify the school or the personnel involved.
- School A is a large secondary school in a major Australian city.
- Importantly, the school is catering for a sizeable low socioeconomic group, which has—as many schools in Australia do—a sizeable proportion of its students with a non-English speaking background.
- Notwithstanding, the students' families were prepared to find the funds to acquire the mobile technology for their children.
- The school is well resourced with technology.
- The school has opted for a standard 1:1 netbook model for Years 7–12 students.
- All students are obliged to use the same model, with the same software configured by the school's ICT team.

BYOT developments

In the later part of 2010, the school gave permission for some Year 12 students to bring their own laptops to class. The next year the principal gave permission for all students to bring their own laptops to class.

That usage was encouraged by a cross-section of the teachers and, in particular, a learning coordinator. However, the move was strongly opposed by the ICT team who insisted that only the common standard set and maintained by them could be used. They were not about to cede any power.

The conflicting approaches came to a head when a special needs student had his personal laptop confiscated by the ICT team and was called arrogant for daring to use his own technology in class. Not surprisingly, there was considerable dissent among the teaching staff, both in relation to the treatment of the student and the inflexible approach adopted by the ICT team.

In brief, the principal had allowed two competing models of personal technology resourcing to go head to head, without making clear to all that one approach would be phased out and another phased in.

The learning coordinator opted to seek employment elsewhere. The special needs student moved to an independent school.

CHAPTER **9**

EVOLUTION AND EFFECTIVENESS

As soon as your implementation plan is underway it is important to ready the school for the inevitable developments that will occur during its use, to ensure the plan does its job and to put in place the processes to measure and refine the effectiveness of your BYOT package. We're suggesting your prime focus should be the transition period leading up to the 100 per cent uptake, reasoning that by that stage BYOT should have been normalised and seamlessly integrated into the school's operations, and as such should then be considered simply as part of the school's overall development strategy.

EVOLUTION

Throughout the transition period, be it two or three years, the scene around you is going to continue to evolve at pace, often in ways that will surprise. It is important in your planning to appreciate that you are but at the beginning of a major development and while we have flagged a seemingly large suite of possible outcomes in Chapter 3, as indicated those options will continue to grow. This will particularly be so with the technology, but you will also find that in going digital and collaborating more closely with your homes and students, the changes will also be evidenced in the everyday workings and teaching of the school.

BYOT will change the way many things are done.

Inevitably as you and your school's community become more familiar with BYOT and aware of the opportunities opened, your expectations and those of the parents and students will continue to rise. The key is to watch the developments in and outside the school and to attune the school's operations accordingly. It is highly likely that the introduction of BYOT will bring with it a batch of unintended outcomes, some of which could significantly impact on the school and its community. Even with the greatest of prescience, it is simply impossible these days to anticipate all the likely outcomes from an initiative as fundamental as this.

In using BYOT and following market forces, you will have largely removed yourself from the hassles and risks associated with maintaining current personal digital technology. Notwithstanding, the school will still need to ensure it can accommodate the ever-emerging technology. Ask anyone trying to accommodate iPads with their link to personal accounts within iTunes to understand the kind of travails that can be experienced.

As indicated in Chapter 7, while the school's wi-fi network will largely resolve the old Windows, Linux and Apple compatibility issues as the technology evolves and the offerings expand, so other issues are likely to emerge.

EFFECTIVENESS

There are two significant areas of effectiveness that have to be addressed and appropriate monitoring processes put in place.

BYOT implementation strategy

The first, and at this stage the key area is the effectiveness of the school's BYOT implementation strategy in achieving 100 per cent student uptake.

The checklists in Chapter 8 mentioned the kind of processes that could be used. You may need to attune elements of the chosen BYOT package to achieve faster—or if desired, slower—uptake. Be conscious that, as with any change of this magnitude, you may well have to spend money in the short term to reap the longer-term savings. It would be wise to have a pool of funds budgeted for this purpose.

Obviously, the sooner you achieve 100 per cent sustained student usage the better, but there may be local factors that oblige the school to move more slowly.

Impact of BYOT

The second and far more complex challenge is examining the impact of BYOT on the school's operations.

The imperative in assessing the impact of your BYOT package is to consider all facets of the school's operations—educational, administrative, organisational and financial—in and outside the school. Importantly, also consider the school's relationship with its community, the students' relationship with their teachers and the impact of the enhanced collaboration on the school's culture.

It is also important that you employ processes that address both the planned and unintended outcomes. It could be argued that one of the great shortcomings of much of the research on the impact of technology on schooling is the propensity to focus on a few planned outcomes and forget the profound unintended outcomes. At times one senses that the researchers, often at a government's behest, are so preoccupied with the minutiae on the ground, they don't recognise that the shape of the forest is changing. It is something to guard against and to ensure at the outset that you get up in the helicopter and view the total scene.

Inevitably there will be calls from government—probably from the day you start your implementation strategy—to comment on the impact of BYOT on student learning, and in particular the learning linked to the formal curriculum. While it is important that you have processes to address the impact on teaching and learning, it is also vital that you consider your context.

If your school already has extensive school-supplied personal technology in each classroom and the students are already making extensive 24/7/365 use of their personal technology, we find it hard to envisage why there would be any significant change in this area simply because of the graduated change in ownership. That said, with total student ownership, the additional trust given the students and the improved student–teacher relationship, in time there might be.

It is suggested that you be ready to respond about that total student-ownership stage and to communicate succinctly where you anticipate the major changes will be occurring. It should also be stressed that the benefits are likely to be found in the education, administration, communication, finances and collaboration between the home and the school. Also make it clear, though, that until the school has achieved near on 100 per cent uptake, many of those changes will not become fully apparent. The key is to ensure that you have processes to assess the impact in all these areas and, as indicated, processes that pick up both the intended and the unintended outcomes.

Based on experience, discussions with the case study schools and the research on collaboration (Lee & Ward, forthcoming), the use of instructional technology in schools (Lee & Winzenried, 2009) and the evolution of networked school communities (Lee & Finger, 2010), our suspicion is that the impact of BYOT is likely to be found in the areas we have listed below, possibly far more than in specific areas of the curriculum.

One of the great challenges you will need to bear in mind when considering the list below and in examining the impact of BYOT on the school's operations will be to clarify which of a probable suite of the variables are having the impact—conscious that it is rarely the technology per se that has the effect but rather, in most instances, how it is used. While, for example, one can safely note that bringing X pieces of technology into the classroom lifts the value of the 'school's' resources by Y per cent, when it comes to exploring the effect of BYOT on the personalisation of the school's teaching there is likely to be a set of other variables at play, possibly facilitated by the introduction of the personal technology.

A particular challenge with BYOT, which we are noting already in the case studies, is whether the impact comes from the use of the personal technology or from the collaboration, particularly between the home and the school and the students and their teachers. The suspicion is that in any instances the key factor will be the enhanced collaboration and a new level of trust.

As indicated in Chapter 5, one needs to be wary of the simplistic 'spins' used by the PR units in governments and companies seeking to take advantage of BYOT. Look instead at these kinds of areas listed below for change and improvements.

More efficient, networked, relevant, attractive and personalised 24/7/365 teaching and learning

- Ability of each student to use their preferred personalised digital office and tools anywhere, any time, 24/7/365
- Incentives to use more student-centred, enquiry-based and personalised teaching
- Ease of teachers facilitating the 24/7/365 use of the networked world by all students

- Instant access to the internet by students anywhere, any time
- Teachers' facility to enhance efficiencies for both themselves and students in working with digital teaching materials

Movement from a strongly insular to a more collaborative and networked mode of teaching and learning

- Ease of all the teachers of young people (classroom teachers, parents, grandparents and young people themselves) and their peers adopting a more collaborative mode of teaching (Lee & Ward, forthcoming)
- Impact upon an evolving school culture, making it more relevant and attractive to all students
- Capacity for older students to lessen their hours of attendance at the place called school
- Freedom for schools to lessen the physical reliance on the insular classroom

Strengthening of home–school collaboration

- Diminution of the home–school divide
- Incentive to provide the owners of the technology with a greater voice in the teaching and operation of the school, and the holistic teaching of each child
- Impact of the enhanced home–school collaboration on the students' learning, and of the school's culture on enhanced academic performance

Impact of each student having responsibility for their own suite of digital technology and its use

- Impact upon the role and size of the school technology support staff

Strengthening of student–teacher relationships

- Increased trust in each student
- Reduction of teacher control of the teaching and learning process
- Enhanced bond between teachers and students
- Greater awareness of each student's preferred learning style

Bridge between in- and out-of-school teaching and learning

- Enhancement of the teachers' understanding of the young people's out-of-school teaching and learning
- Facility to refresh the school's paper-based model of teaching and learning and to evolve one that is more appropriate for a networked world

School community's sustained use of 'state of the art' technology

- Impact within the classroom, the home and on the move
- Complementarity with the use of school-funded technology
- Reduction of duplication of personal technology and waste
- Diminution of risk from poor choice, with greater reliance on the marketplace
- Facility for the school to focus its attention on the core, less changeable infrastructure

Change in the school technology resourcing model

- Shift away from the idea that government has to fund, and indeed provide, all the personal technology in the school
- Adoption of a more collaborative public/private/community school technology resourcing model
- Extent of the recurrent contribution of the BYOT technology—hardware and software—to the school's resources
- Possible facility to reduce ICT support budget/staffing
- Recurrent savings for the school after expenses
- Resources able to be redeployed

Impact of home–school collaboration on school resourcing

- Increased teaching resources—human and capital—emerging out of collaboration with homes (Lee & Ward, forthcoming)
- Recurrent capital increase emanating from improved home–school collaboration

School's administration efficiencies

- Role of the technology in facilitating the enhanced effectiveness and efficiency of school administration, organisation and communication, as well the organisation of the students' daily life
- Savings from moving from paper-based to digital communication
- Shift to more efficient, inexpensive and integrated digitally based operations

Productivity

- Role played by BYOT technology in increasing efficiencies, economies and synergy
- Synergies made possible with the total school community's normalised use of the digital

We would also suggest that you consider the impact of BYOT upon the lives of young people, the pleasure, value and learning the technology brings to them, both in and outside the classroom, the likely impact on their attitude and approach to their ongoing learning and development as a person, as well as the likely impact on their learning of the academic.

Tapscott (2009) documents in *Growing up digital* the profound impact young people's use of their digital technology has had upon their lives and society, to the extent of subtitling his work *How the net generation is changing our world*. Conscious that BYOT is an extension of that development, and with young people now taking their personal technology into one of the last bastions of the old ways—the classroom, one should expect a similar impact.

We would strongly urge that you document the financial contribution that BYOT and the associated closer collaboration with the parents brings to the school, both in the way of additional resources and the kind of funds and resourcing it enables the school to redeploy. One would expect your government to be searching out those figures in the near future.

CONCLUSION

We mentioned at the beginning of the book our concern about the naive simplicity of so many of the current comments about BYOT, the microfocus on the technology per se and the imperative of getting a helicopter view in considering every facet of the school's operations and where the astute use of BYOT can enhance the school's performance. That holds equally when watching the ever-evolving scene, evaluating the effectiveness of your BYOT implementation strategy and assessing the impact of BYOT on the school, both inside the school walls and upon the school's community.

While the media—and, sadly, the politicians—like the simplistic sound grabs, the reality is that in BYOT you are addressing a development that should be integrated into an ever-more complex human organisation where a host of variables need to be borne in mind. You are also talking about impact in an ever-changing organisation with an ever-evolving technology.

ST MARY STAR OF THE SEA COLLEGE

Situation

- St Mary Star of the Sea College is an independent Catholic girls' college situated in Wollongong, New South Wales, Australia. Wollongong is a major coastal city approximately an hour's drive south of Sydney.
- Overlooking the ocean, this long-established school caters for approximately 1100 girls in Years 7–12.
- As an independent school, it has total control over its own operations, its staff selection and the allocation of its resources.
- The student group is socioeconomically well above the Australian norm, with all students having ready access to the internet at home and a diversity of personal technology.

Fuller details on the school and its program can be found at:
https://www.stmarys.nsw.edu.au/.
Contact: Frank Pitt, Principal

BYOT developments

Interestingly, St Mary is one of two independent schools in Wollongong that have begun the move along the BYOT path. The other is The Illawarra Grammar School (p. 122).

As with many of the other case study schools, the move to BYOT at St Mary flowed naturally from the school's normalised use of the digital and the seeming ease of making far better use of the girls' personal technology.

The school was well equipped technology-wise, running a 1:1 Windows-based computing program, having all teaching rooms with the appropriate technology, all staff being provided with laptops and a critical mass of teachers using the digital in their teaching. It was, however, a 'one size fits all' approach that banned the use of the students' mobile technology.

The principal questioned the educational validity of the old approach and the seemingly unnecessary block on the use of the personal technology that the girls use 24/7/365. He thus decided to let the girls start using their own technology in 2010, without any fanfare. From the outset the students were responsible for the care and maintenance of their own technology.

The principal also decided to trial the use of iPads in the senior school, a not insignificant change in a Windows school. All the staff were provided with iPads before the trial started.

Vitally, the principal has opted to build on the natural emergence of BYOT, not to overplan an as yet little-understood development, to let BYOT evolve and take its own form, only every so often giving it an occasional nudge.

The leadership has been willing to cede some of the traditional planning control. That said, it has opted to use an acceptable-use policy with BYOT that the girls have to sign.

The school is well aware of the general direction in which it wants to move and how it should support the girls and the staff in that movement, but it recognises it has the time to let the development take its own course.

THE ILLAWARRA GRAMMAR SCHOOL

Situation

- The Illawarra Grammar School (TIGS) is an independent coeducational school situated in Wollongong, New South Wales, Australia. Wollongong is a major coastal city approximately an hour's drive south of Sydney.
- This well-established school, with strong Anglican Church links, caters for approximately 1000 students from Kindergarten to Year 12.
- As an independent school it has total control over its own operations, its staff selection and the allocation of its resources.

- The student group is socioeconomically well above the Australian norm, with all students having ready access to the internet at home and a diversity of personal technology.

Fuller details on the school and its program can be found at:
http://www.tigs.nsw.edu.au/.
Contact: Leanne Windsor, Director of Information Services

BYOT developments

Interestingly, Illawarra Grammar is one of two independent schools in Wollongong that have begun the move along the BYOT path. The other is St Mary Star of the Sea College (see p. 121).

The move to BYOT at TIGS was prompted by the desire of the principal, Stephen Kinsella, to provide an education more appropriate for the twenty-first century and the reality that a significant part of the school's technology resources would be taken out of play in 2012 by a major school rebuilding program. The principal, although conscious that a sizeable proportion of the teachers had not normalised the use of the digital in their teaching, believed it was nonetheless an opportune time for the school and the students in Years 7–12 to make the move to a BYOT model.

The school put the onus on the families of the senior students to provide the desired mobile technology for their children. Aware of the need to transition from the old to the new as seamlessly as possible, the school opted to continue to provide the requisite specialist technology. Fuller details of the school's approach can be found at: http://www.tigs.nsw.edu.au/index.php?option=com_content&view=article&id=847&Itemid=668.

To assist the school in making the move it appointed a new Director of Information Services to oversee the new approach, lead a new iCentre and ensure that all the requisite infrastructure and systems were in place, policies were readied and staff and students were supported.

What impresses with the TIGS move, like that of virtually all the other case studies, is the recognition that it was time for the school to make the move, an immense excitement about what was to happen and a strong commitment by the leadership to ensure that the journey through the unchartered territory was well prepared.

CHAPTER **10**

THE CHALLENGES AHEAD

RECOGNISING AND UNDERSTANDING THE BYOT IMPLICATIONS

Our desire in writing this book was to open the eyes to all in the school community—the parents, students, staff and school leadership, plus those many others that support the school in the local area and central offices—of the profound implications of a school moving to allow the students to bring their own technology into the teaching room. While at first glance BYOT might appear to be a simple move, our hope is that we will have alerted you to the game-changing implications of the development and the desirability of the total school community and educational administrators understanding what is entailed in the move. The case study schools are already providing an insight into the impact BYOT is likely to have upon the nature of schooling, teaching, instructional technology used, the school technology support model, administration of the school, relationship between the school and its homes and resourcing of schools in a networked world.

The resourcing implications are potentially immense, for BYOT has the facility to move the resourcing of state schools away from the time-honoured model where government provided (or was perceived as providing) all the school's resources to one where the parents, the local civic and business community and government all contribute to the resourcing of the school. The important point to grasp is that there are lessons to be learned from those pathfinding schools across the developed world that have in their introduction of BYOT already begun (albeit yet in a very small way) fundamental resourcing changes that BYOT engenders.

Historically, many teachers and education academics have shown little interest in the economics of resourcing a school, tending to leave that area to the accountants and the bureaucrats. BYOT is likely to help change that outlook and to have all involved in the school better appreciate how this initiative simultaneously impacts on the educational, social, organisational, technological and financial development of the school.

It is thus important in introducing BYOT to swiftly quash the notion that it is simply a technical development and to actively promote an understanding by all in the school and its immediate community of the many potential opportunities opened, and how those opportunities can significantly enhance and change the workings of the school in many areas. An appreciation of the magnitude of the development occurring should assist with the implementation planning at every stage.

It is also important to understand that the development is wholly consistent with the developments elsewhere in life and in the workplace and that, as with those developments, it is an inevitability that needs to be shaped astutely if the desired outcomes are to be achieved.

WHOLE SCHOOL COMMUNITY NORMALISATION

A key feature of those societal and workplace developments is the normalised use of the digital. All, from the leaders of the land—the presidents and prime ministers—through to the toddlers, now use the digital every day in their lives. The use of the digital is all-pervasive virtually everywhere except in the classroom.

It is an anomaly that needs be redressed swiftly. It is fundamental to achieving and sustaining 100 per cent BYOT uptake and for the development to become a normal facet of contemporary schooling.

While the students and most parents have normalised digital use, until all the teachers in the school have done so in their teaching the school won't achieve 100 per cent BYOT usage. Achieve total teacher normalisation and not only will the school be on course to achieve the desired outcomes but, vitally, it will also be on course for the staff to adopt a networked mindset and genuinely collaborate with the students and their homes.

THE CHALLENGE FOR THE EARLY MOVERS

As flagged, getting the school and its immediate community—the leadership, teachers, students and parents—to view the introduction of BYOT from a networked mindset, and not from the traditional insular mindset, is crucial. The changing of that mindset will take time, but the more the educators learn to genuinely collaborate with their school's community, the sooner it will evolve and ever-more potential opportunities will be likely to emerge.

We readily appreciate there are few if any schools that have reached the point of achieving 100 per cent normalised use of the students' technology. The newness of the development will for some time make the challenge for the pathfinders that much greater. You will inevitably have to educate all who impact on your school's operations on the reasons for and the nature and implications of the move. Of course, there will be some who are reluctant to leave the old ways and abandon their power base; that could well happen at both the school and authority level.

That said, the global interest in the development and the swift recognition by many of its considerable benefits could soon overcome those doubters. It was, for example, interesting to note the dramatic uptake in interest in Forsyth County's BYOT 'expo' between 2011 and 2012, and the number of states and nations attending in 2012.

Another of the challenges associated with moving early is that inevitably you are going to move into unchartered territory where you will have to rely on your own acumen. One of the major differences between organisations when they go digital is that they move from a world of relative constancy and continuity where much the same happens each year and all know what to expect, to one of ongoing evolution and change and, vitally, where all in the organisation are obliged to move into areas where few or none have moved before. This will happen with your school's introduction of BYOT.

While we have shared with you the learning experience of the pathfinders, your particular situation may mean some aspect of the approach is not applicable and that you will move into the unknown with no guide, where the school and its community are going to have to use their own nous to identify the best way forward. We'd suggest it would be wise to make this situation clear to your school community. Unashamedly declare that you don't have all the answers, stress that you would appreciate their input, adopt a flexible implementation strategy and be ready to vary your approach as the feedback and need require.

The digital makes it easy to instantly and inexpensively communicate with and secure the thoughts of all in your school community.

HOME–SCHOOL COLLABORATION

The authors appreciate that genuine and open home–school collaboration is likely to be a significant change for most schools and that it will take time and deed to demonstrate the authenticity of the school's intentions. It is a nebulous variable you will need to bear in mind in your planning. Some of you might virtually overnight be moving from an all-out ban of the gear to a position where you are encouraging the students to use the technology in class.

The students and parents may well be rightly sceptical. Sadly it only takes one adverse comment or the action of one casual teacher to set your BYOT aspirations back appreciably.

That said, set yourself the target of achieving total normalised use of the students' technology in every class as soon as is possible, but be realistic in shaping the school's implementation plan and the indicative implementation time line. As indicated, each school has to gauge from the local variables how long it will take from the introduction of BYOT to its 100 per cent uptake. Some schools might never reach that position, particularly if BYOT is approached without due regard to the many key factors discussed in the earlier pages.

Hopefully by now it is clear that the successful normalised use of BYOT entails all the members of the school community working together. It is most assuredly not a job just for a committee or an ICT team, no matter how brilliant. For BYOT to realise the desired outcomes it must be thoughtfully and seamlessly woven into the total fabric of the networked school community. It has to be naturally factored into all the school's planning and operations from the beginning, so that in time the model will become invisible and a natural part of the school's operations.

BYOT PACKAGE

A vital part of the total solution will be the BYOT package you choose and its acceptability to the parents and students.

As mentioned, the current literature addresses BYOT primarily from a teacher's perspective and how readily the teachers will accept the model, not the clients. We'd like to stress that it would make appreciably more sense to address the introduction of BYOT primarily through the eyes of those being asked to provide their personal technology. In brief, how would you as a parent or student react to the model chosen, and would you consider supporting the classroom use of that technology?

READINESS

Another key element that should strongly influence the school's BYOT strategy and the indicative implementation time line is its readiness to introduce the initiative. As stressed throughout, unless your school has the desired base on which to build, all the signs are that you will struggle to get more than incidental student use.

As indicated, while you cannot always work with the ideal in your planning, make sure that all the variables are eventually addressed, because until that remediation is done progress will be limited. This need to ensure a strong platform on which to build, which is the kind of situation a new principal could encounter when taking over a school.

As stressed, your BYOT implementation strategy has to be just that: one suited to your particular situation. The case studies and the associated organisational change research can provide important guidance, but that is all they can do. Each school has to identify an approach it believes will work best. While ideally it would help to have the support of one's local authority and the national government in the early days, you shouldn't bank on it; rather, you're more likely to encounter opposition. Similarly, each school has to make the call to finetune or vary its approach if the feedback is showing shortcomings.

In time you will be able to turn to other colleagues and consultants like us for advice.

OUTCOMES

In your planning, be conscious of the main outcomes you want to realise, but also be aware that as your understanding of BYOT grows you are likely to add others and that there are likely to be significant unintended outcomes. Historically, far too often educators have sought out only what they want from the technology, even if it is not likely to be there, largely dismissing many of the unintended positive outcomes. Don't make that mistake. Take advantage of and seek to enhance all the outcomes that assist in the holistic education of the young.

BYOT IMPLEMENTATION

The more we examined the key variables needing to be addressed to achieve the desired student uptake, and the more we recognised how far off many schools still are from normalising the whole-of-staff use of the digital, the more we saw the imperative of an astute BYOT implementation strategy, constantly finetuned by a regular flow of student acceptance data. Schools, even those ready to make the move, are going to have to work hard and be clever over a concerted period to achieve the desired level of student uptake.

The principal has no option other than to lead that implementation. Granted, the executive team also has to play a key role, but the principal must lead, provide direction, supply political acumen and overcome the inevitable frustrations and hurdles. As indicated, the school has to measure the monthly uptake and regularly assess the effectiveness of its strategy.

Getting teachers to use a teaching approach that encourages all students to bring their own technology could in many situations be extremely hard to achieve and may in reality have to wait until those teachers retire.

BYOT IMPACT

While the prime focus in the transition stage should be on total student usage, appropriate consideration should also start to be given to the impact of BYOT on the various school operations and its relationship with its community, tracking those developments as the percentage of users grows.

As indicated at the outset, our focus has been to address why your school should make the move to a model of BYOT and to advise how you might best set about moving into the new territory. In examining the work of the pathfinders, while there are hints of emerging trends, it is still too early to comment on the impact of BYOT and the potentially disparate technologies on the nature or indeed the effectiveness of the teaching. One of the challenges will be to identify which developments can be attributed to BYOT and which flow from the closer home–school collaboration.

Notwithstanding, from early in your journey you will begin to notice changes, and those changes you should document. With this in mind, the authors have already embarked on researching and writing a follow-up work that will in essence examine, through case studies, BYOT in action. Until we have schools where a critical mass of the students are using their own personal technology in class, we will refrain from commenting on how much of the theory discussed in Chapter 3 works out in practice.

CONCLUSION

In our work with the case study schools and an education authority like Forsyth County, which are experiencing the dividends that flowed naturally from normalising the use of the digital and which were collaborating with their homes, the enduring images that emerged were the naturalness of the development, the pride in what they had achieved, but also the realisation that they had only begun to reap the benefits of the development. The contrast with those case study schools that chose to introduce BYOT from 'on high' was pronounced, with all flagging major issues relating to the school's readiness which they appreciate are going to be difficult to rectify.

As indicated at the outset, BYOT is a development that eventually every school will take on board. The forces and rationale impelling the move are too powerful to avoid. Your challenge is to identify as a parent, student, teacher or educational administrator how the school can shape our young people's all-pervasive use of their personal technology to the best advantage.

BIBLIOGRAPHY

Australian Communications and Media Authority (ACMA) 2007, *Media and communications in Australian families*, ACMA, Canberra. Available from http://www.acma.gov.au/webwr/_assets/main/lib101058/media_and_society_report_2007.pdf.

Becta 2008, *Extending opportunity*, final report of the Minister's Taskforce on home access to technology, Becta, Coventry.

Becta 2009a, *Harnessing technology for next generation learning: Children, schools and families implementation plan 2009–2012*, Becta, Coventry.

Becta 2009b, *Home Access presentation*, Becta, Coventry.

Bellanca, J & Brandt, R 2010, *21st Century skills: Rethinking how students learn*, Solution Tree Press, Bloomington.

Berthelsen, D 2010, 'Support at home increases chance of school success'. Available from http://insciences.org/article.php?article_id=2319.

Betcher, C & Lee, M 2009, *The interactive whiteboard revolution: Teaching with IWBs*, ACER Press, Camberwell.

Cassell, J & Cramer, M 2008, 'High tech or high risk: Moral panics about girls online', in T. McPherson (ed.), *Digital youth, innovation, and the unexpected*, The John D. and Catherine T. MacArthur Foundation Series on Digital Media and Learning, The MIT Press, pp. 53–76. Available from http://www.mitpressjournals.org/doi/abs/10.1162/dmal.9780262633598.053.

Chowdry, H, Crawford, C & Goodman, A 2009, *Drivers and barriers to educational success: Evidence from the longitudinal study of young people in England*, Institute for Fiscal Studies DCSF–RR102, Department for Education, UK.

Cisco 2011, *Cisco Visual Networking Index: Forecast and methodology 2010-2015*. Available from http://www.cisco.com/en/US/solutions/collateral/ns341/ns525/ns537/ns705/ns827/white_paper_c11-481360_ns827_Networking_Solutions_White_Paper.html.

comScore 2011, 'More than 200 billion online videos viewed globally in October'. Press release, comScore Video Metrix. Available from http://www.comscore.com/Press_Events/Press_Releases/2011/12/YouTube_Accounts_for_At_Least_34_Percent_of_All_Videos.

Cuban, L 1986, *Teachers and machines: The classroom use of technology since 1920*, Teachers College Press, New York.

Desforges, C & Abouchaar, A 2003, *The impact of parental involvement, parent support and family education on pupil achievement and adjustment: A literature review*, Department for Education and Science, Nottingham, UK.

Dewey, J 1916, *Democracy and education*, Macmillan, New York.

eSchool News staff writers 2010 (February), 'Experts: Schools can track laptop use less expensively', *eSchool News*.

eSchool News staff writers 2011 (October), 'Inside a "Bring Your Own Device" program', *eSchool News*.

Estyn 2009, *Good practice in parental involvement in primary schools—April 2009*, Her Majesty's Inspectorate for Education and Training, Cardiff, Wales.

Fisher, D 2012, 'BYOT' blog: http://www.scoop.it/byot.

Friedman, T 2006, *The world is flat*, 2nd edn, Farrar, Straus Giroux, New York.

Grant, D 1989, *Learning relations*, Routledge, London.

Grant, L 2010 (August), *Developing the home–school relationship using digital technologies*, Futurelab.

Green, H & Hannon, C 2007, *Their space: Education for a digital generation*, Demos, London.

Hattie, J 2009, *Visible learning*, Routledge, London.

Hobson, J 2012, unpublished communication with author.

Illinois Institute of Design 2007, *Schools in the digital age*, Illinois Institute of Technology.

Ito, M, Horst, H, Bittanti, M, Boyd, D, Herr-Stephenson, B, Lange, P, Pascoe, C & Robinson, L 2008, *Living and learning with new media: Summary of findings from the Digital Youth Project*, The John D. and Catherine T. Macarthur Foundation Reports on Digital Media and Learning. Available from http://digitalyouth.ischool.berkeley.edu/files/report/digitalyouth-WhitePaper.pdf.

Korngold, S 2012, unpublished communication with author.

Lee, M 1996, 'The educated home', *The Practising Administrator*, vol. 18, no. 3.

Lee, M & Finger, G (eds) 2010, *Developing a networked school community: A guide to realising the vision*, ACER Press, Camberwell.

Lee, M & Gaffney, M 2008, *Leading a digital school*, ACER Press, Camberwell.

Lee, M & Levins, M 2010, 'Homes and the digital technology: A home–school difference or digital divide?', in M Lee & G Finger (eds), *Developing a networked school community: A guide to realising the vision*, ACER Press, Camberwell.

Lee, M & Ryall, B 2010, 'Financing the networked school community: Building upon the home investment', in M Lee & G Finger (eds), *Developing a networked school community: A guide to realising the vision*, ACER Press, Camberwell.

Lee, M & Ward, L forthcoming, *Beyond four walls: Embracing collaboration in learning* (working title), ACER Press, Camberwell.

Lee, M & Winzenried, A 2009, *The use of instructional technology in schools: Lessons to be learned*, ACER Press, Camberwell.

Lipnack, J & Stamps, J 1994, *The age of the network: Organizing principles for the 21st century*, John Wiley & Sons, Inc., New York.

Mackenzie, J 2009, *Family learning: Engaging with parents*, Dunedin Academic Press, Edinburgh.

Maher, D & Lee, M 2010, 'Student Internet access in a networked school community: The challenge', in M Lee & G Finger (eds), *Developing a networked school community: A guide to realising the vision*, ACER Press, Camberwell.

Meredyth, D, Russell, N, Blackwood, L, Thomas, J & Wise, P. 1998, *Real time: Computers, change and schooling*, Department of Education, Training and Youth Affairs, Canberra. Available from http://www.dest.gov.au/archive/schools/Publications/1999/realtime.pdf.

Mitchell, B 2012, unpublished interview.

Naismith, L, Lonsdale, P, Vavoula, G & Sharples, M 2006, *Literature review in mobile technologies and learning*, Futurelab Series Report 11, Futurelab, Bristol.

NMC 2011, *Horizon Report 2011 K–12 Edition*, New Media Consortium, California.

Perelman, L 1992, *School's out*, Avon Books, New York.

Project Tomorrow 2010, *Unleashing the future: Educators 'speak up' about the use of emerging technologies for learning*, Speak Up May 2010, Project Tomorrow. www.tomorrow.org.

Project Tomorrow 2011, *The new three E's of education: Enabled, engaged and empowered.* Speak Up 2010 National Findings, Project Tomorrow. www.tomorrow.org.

Project Tomorrow 2012, *Personalizing the classroom experience: Teachers, librarians and administrators connect the dots with digital learning*, Speak Up 2001 National Findings, May 2012, Project Tomorrow. www.tomorrow.org.

Shirky, C 2008, *Here comes everybody: Organizing without organizations*, Penguin, New York.

Speirs, F 2010 (October), 'Run what ya brung'. Available from http://speirs.org/blog/2010/10/9/run-what-ya-brung.html.

Stager, G 2012, 'BYOD—worst idea of the 21st Century?' Available from http://stager.tv/blog/?p=2397.

Strom, RD & Strom, PS 2010, *Parenting young children: Exploring the Internet, play and reading*, Information Age Publishing, Charlotte.

Tapscott, D 1998, *Growing up digital: The rise of the Net Generation*, McGraw Hill, New York.

Tapscott, D 2009, *Grown up digital: How the Net Generation is changing our world*, McGraw Hill, New York.

Tolley, R 2010, 'UK Home Access Program: A case study', in M Lee & G Finger (eds), *Developing a networked school community: A guide to realising the vision*, ACER Press, Camberwell.

Traxler, J 2010a, 'Will student devices deliver innovation, inclusion and transformation?', *Journal of the Research Centre for Educational Technology*, vol. 6, no. 1.

Traxler, J 2010b (March), 'Ramblings' blog. Available from http://profjohntraxler.blogspot.com/.

Ward, L, Parr, JM & Robinson, VMJ 2005, 'Limited use, limited impact: The ICT dilemma', paper presented at the Annual Meeting of the American Educational Research Association, Montreal, Canada.

Windsor, L 2012, 'BYOD or BYOT @ school' blog. Available from http://www.scoop.it/t/byod.

INDEX